Praise for *Creating Positive Classroom Climates*

"Now more than ever before, it is clear that educators have to be flexible and ready for anything. *Creating Positive Classroom Climates* is timely and relevant, offering a plethora of tools and strategies which are applicable to every classroom. It is the book teachers need to rethink and restructure what learning can look like, and it is written by teachers for teachers. If you've ever been afraid to try something new or to re-envision what learning can look like in your classroom, this is the book for you!"—**Lindsey L. Jensen, 2018 Illinois Teacher of the Year, Educators Rising Illinois State Coordinator**

"*Creating Positive Classroom Climate* is a practical and comprehensive book that benefits all educators. The book supports both the novice teacher and the reflective educator at any stage or level of their career. The area of culture and climate is at the foundation of *good teaching*. When I meet with teachers, I often ask, 'What is in YOUR toolbox?' If there is any question or doubt, this essential read will poignantly help them find and utilize the strategies, instructional skills, and pedagogically sound techniques to develop and maintain a positive classroom climate climate in the classroom. As a former teacher, reading coach, vice principal, a principal coach, and as a sitting principal, I believe this book will help lead to robust conversations about teaching and learning."—**Paula Bethea, M.A., principal, Trenton, NJ**

"At a time when our students have more non-academic needs than ever before, it is critical that every educator has tools to support their students (and themselves). In this book, Maureen and Jonathan lay out exactly what to consider when determining how to support students and strategies to meet them where they are, all through the lens of research involving teachers in diverse settings. What a gift! Dive in, implement, and watch the magic happen."—**LaVonna Roth, founder, consultant, and lead speaker of Ignite Your S.H.I.N.E.**

Creating Positive
Classroom Climate

About *Building Your Teaching Toolbox* Series

We chose to name this series *Building Your Teaching Toolbox* because we think a toolbox is a strong metaphor for becoming an effective educator. New teachers enter the profession with a toolbox that needs to be filled with strategies they can try out and practice to determine which are their go-to tools. Veteran teachers often have a teaching toolbox filled with some tools that are well-worn and others that might be in need of revitalizing or updating to make them more efficient, fun to use, and thus, more useful for students.

The importance of a well-filled toolbox is not something we take lightly as educators with nearly a half-century of teaching combined under our belts; we continue to revisit our tools to figure out what needs to be updated and consider new strategies to add that enhance our pedagogy. Each district, school, classroom, and child is different, and from year to year, whether or not a teacher changes schools, tools a teacher uses need to be adapted to meet the needs of the new students they are teaching. Therefore, our book series is focused on *Building Your Teaching Toolbox* to support new teachers in developing practical teaching strategies they can adapt for any school context and to support veteran teachers in revitalizing and adding to their already established teaching toolbox.

Within this series, readers will find tried and tested teaching strategies that can be turnkeyed for any school context. The strategies in each book are developed from successful K–12 teachers from across the US and globally. In attempting to create a book that would provide a comprehensive number of teaching tools to fill a teacher's toolbox, we realized one book would not suffice. This led to the creation of the five-book *Building Your Teaching Toolbox* Book Series that provides 30 strategies in each of four focus areas: (1) classroom climate; (2) planning; (3) instruction; and (4) professional development. The first book in the series provides five core strategies in each of these four areas, and each subsequent book is focused on one pedagogical area at a time (book 2: classroom climate; book 3: planning; book 4: instruction; and book 5: professional development).

Having taught and supervised students in so many different school contexts, we knew this book series needed to emphasize how to modify core strategies in multiple ways. Therefore, every teaching strategy throughout the book series includes tips on how to adapt the strategy based on grade level, type of learner, and different school assets and needs such as class size, technology, and cultural diversity.

Along with these adaptations, we wanted to be sure that readers could imagine what strategy implementation might be like in their classrooms. Each strategy comes alive through the stories of how contributing teachers have used and adapted the strategies they shared. We also recognize that one great strategy actually requires numerous tiny strategies to effectively execute; so we break down each strategy like nesting dolls where readers will see the overall larger strategy and then more and more details are revealed that will help readers make the strategy their own.

We believe the *Building Your Teaching Toolbox* series will serve as a practical resource for educators of all backgrounds and experience while also helping to create a toolbox community where we can continue to learn and grow from one another. Thanks for becoming part of that community!

Creating Positive Classroom Climate

30 Practical Strategies for All School Contexts

Maureen Connolly
Jonathan Ryan Davis

ROWMAN & LITTLEFIELD
Lanham • Boulder • New York • London

Published by Rowman & Littlefield
An imprint of The Rowman & Littlefield Publishing Group, Inc.
4501 Forbes Boulevard, Suite 200, Lanham, Maryland 20706
www.rowman.com

86-90 Paul Street, London EC2A 4NE, United Kingdom

Copyright © 2022 by Jonathan Ryan Davis and Maureen Connolly

All rights reserved. No part of this book may be reproduced in any form or by any electronic or mechanical means, including information storage and retrieval systems, without written permission from the publisher, except by a reviewer who may quote passages in a review.

British Library Cataloguing in Publication Information Available

Library of Congress Cataloging-in-Publication Data

Names: Connolly, Maureen (English teacher), author. | Davis, Jonathan Ryan, author.
Title: Creating positive classroom climate : 30 practical strategies for all school contexts / Maureen Connolly and Jonathan Ryan Davis.
Description: Lanham : Rowman & Littlefield, [2022] | Series: Building your teaching toolbox | Includes bibliographical references. | Summary: "In this book, you will learn how practicing teachers in diverse school and classroom contexts have implemented successful strategies to create and maintain a positive classroom climate that enables ALL students to thrive"—Provided by publisher.
Identifiers: LCCN 2022014019 (print) | LCCN 2022014020 (ebook) | ISBN 9781475849752 (cloth) | ISBN 9781475849769 (paperback) | ISBN 9781475849776 (epub)
Subjects: LCSH: Classroom environment. | Teacher-student relationships.
Classification: LCC LB3013 .D396 2022 (print) | LCC LB3013 (ebook) | DDC 371.102/4—dc23/eng/20220526
LC record available at https://lccn.loc.gov/2022014019
LC ebook record available at https://lccn.loc.gov/2022014020

Contents

Foreword		ix
Acknowledgments		xi
Introduction		1
1	**Highlights from *Adaptable Teaching***	9
	Strategy 1: Group Agreements	10
	Strategy 2: Establishing Routines	12
	Strategy 3: Positive Affirmations	14
	Strategy 4: Failing Forward	16
	Strategy 5: Critical Feedback Surveys	18
2	**Getting Started**	21
	Strategy 6: Room Setup	23
	Strategy 7: Getting to Know Students	31
	Strategy 8: Team-Building Games	42
3	**Routines**	57
	Strategy 9: Classroom Jobs	60
	Strategy 10: Check-Ins	67
	Strategy 11: Student Voice to Start Class	73
	Strategy 12: Working the Room	81
	Strategy 13: Brain and Body Breaks	90
	Strategy 14: Mindfulness	97
	Strategy 15: Spotlighting Students	104
4	**Supporting a Positive, Productive Climate**	111
	Strategy 16: Building Positive Teacher-Student Relationships and Trust	113
	Strategy 17: Building Positive Peer-to-Peer Relationships and Trust	118
	Strategy 18: Guiding Students to Share Their Thinking and Feelings	128
	Strategy 19: Connecting through Current Events	134
	Strategy 20: Supporting Student-Led Learning	143
5	**10 Bonus Strategies**	153

Conclusion 157
References 159
Index 161

Foreword

Annie Dillard says, "The way we spend our days is the way we spend our lives." What's true for life is also true to the classroom. We can tell students (and ourselves) what we value, but how we spend our time *shows* our students what we value. And what we most value are the very things that take the *most* time, the things that can't be checked off by a cluster of lesson plans or "three easy steps." Engagement. Trust. Community. These are the rewards we earn by doing the hardest, most unpredictable work: the human work.

Rule #1 about human work is it takes the time it takes. If I didn't know this from living, I've certainly learned it from the classroom. It wasn't too long ago, I had a student, "Katie," in one of my high school English classes. She was petite, yet strong; an accomplished cheerleader. She commanded a presence with the social capital she worked like her platform tennis shoes. There was also something fierce in her eyes, a fearlessness I felt during the first minute she entered the classroom and looked straight at me. Unlike most teenagers on the first day of school who quickly look away or cover their awkwardness with a smile, Katie was looking for something behind my eyes, but I had no idea what.

A younger version of my teacher-self would have been intimidated, but with over two decades behind me, I found myself curious, wondering, and grateful I had learned the value of deep patience. You know, the kind of patience where you trust that time will reveal what you need to learn. Of course, the waiting is seldom smooth and this relationship was no exception. Katie was tough. She'd wait until I would start class and then take her phone out. She openly criticized everything we read, everything we did, every assignment. I knew she hated this class and was pretty certain she hated me, too.

A couple of months into this difficult routine of her criticism and my consistent responses that always started with, "I'm so glad you asked that question" or "Tell me more about what's not working for you," I was losing confidence that we'd find our way. Then one day, we were working on the draft of a paper and she was stuck. I found her hiding in a corner, her frustration visible. We looked at each other, and in that moment, I finally saw Katie. I saw her need for perfection and how her criticisms had been about her fears, not her fortitude. I saw how all of the cell phone acts of resistance and eye rolls and deep sighs had been protecting herself, not punishing me. I sat down beside her on the floor and asked again, "Tell me more about what's not working for you."

"I'm stuck. Can't you see I'm stuck?!" she sighed.

"Yes, I can. Let's put the paper and the tablet away. Can you just talk to me about why it's a bad writing prompt? What do you really want to say?" And so it began. A little crack of a conversation that slowly started to soften everything else. Until eventually, the phone rarely came out. The eye rolls stopped and were replaced by gentle smiles. And on the last day of class a big hug and a soft "thank you."

I wish there was some magic I could share right now, but creating the context for engaged students is always more complex than that. What I can do, though, is share what Katie affirmed for me about this human work of creating classroom spaces where community can thrive.

- **Be curious**. Rather than being angry about acts of resistance, we need to address them and simultaneously be curious about them. There is always a reason for the behaviors we see and curiosity keeps us open to the cracks that reveal more about why.
- **Be patient.** I'm talking *deep* patience here. The kind of patience where you don't see results or changes for months, sometimes. The more curious you stay, the more likely you are to rely on patience as a creator of space. Deep patience isn't the absence of boundaries. I had to tell Katie 100 times to put her phone away before she did it on her own. Deep patience is firm, but consistent.
- **Be consistent.** We can't change other humans. But we can create spaces for them to change themselves. Whether it's through boundaries, natural consequences, or affirmations, we can be consistent about the words we choose and the ways we respond.

This story turned out well. Not all of them do. Yet, we do this messy, complex, human work over and over for those times it ends with that "thank you." As you embark on reading this book from Maureen and Jonathan, I hope you do so with your own Katie in mind. As you learn about strategies and think about community, as you embrace affirmations and reflect on collaboration, I hope you will see their ideas as your stepping stones to this ever-so-precious human endeavor we call teaching.

Sarah Brown Wessling, NBCT
2010 National Teacher of the Year
Senior Advisor of the National Teacher of the Year Program

Acknowledgments

We are incredibly grateful to all of the teachers who contributed to this book. Our conversations with them were insightful and inspiring, and we are glad to be able to share their teacher moves with you. Each contributor is listed at the start of the chapter that they helped form. We also want to recognize all contributors together, here at the start of this book. We are proud to say that four contributors are a former State Teacher of the Year (denoted with an * next to their name).

Thomas (TJ) Belasco, Lower Cape May Regional High School (NJ), 9th–12th grades
Robert Boyce, West Windsor-Plainsboro High School North (NJ), 9th–12th grades
Revathi Balakrishnan,* Elsa England Elementary (TX), 5th grade
Anthony Cianciarulo, Grace A. Dunn Middle School (NJ), 7th–8th grades
Jennifer Podolak Cline, Fisher Middle School (NJ), 8th grade
Sarah Cullom, Dublin Elementary School (CA), 4th grade
Andrew Curtin, Bishop Ireton High School (VA), 11th–12th grades
Brenda Bokenyi, César Chávez Elementary School (OR), 1st grade
Mary Eldredge-Sandbo,* Des-Lacs Burlington High School (ND), 10th–12th grades
Bob Feurer,* North Bend Central Middle School/High School (NE), 7th, 11th–12th grades
Emma First, Delran High School (NJ), 9th–12th grades
Kristen Frade, Mary McDowell Friends School (NY), Kindergarten–1st grades
Pamela Goff, Hedgepeth-Williams Middle School (NJ), 7th grade
Jordan Griffiths, The American School of Kuwait (Kuwait), 3rd grade
Marissa Herrera, Coronado Elementary School (AZ), 3rd grade
Adam Klempa, American School of Paris (France), 9th–12th grades
Alyssa Landy, Luria Academy (NY), 4th–5th grades
Daniel Leija,* Carson Elementary Northside ISD (TX), Kindergarten–5th grades
Ryan McCamy, Trenton Central High School (NJ), 10th–12th grades
Larissa McElrath, Millstone River Elementary School (NJ), 4th grade
Ann Neary, Staples High School (CT), 10th–12th grades
Marta O'Brien, Guardian Angels Catholic School (FL), 6th–8th grades
Jennifer Raser, Wheatland High School (WY), 9th–12th grades

Mindy Resnick, Mary Emily Bryan Middle School (MO), 7th–8th grade
Allison Snyder, Bernards High School (NJ), 9th–12th grades
Kate Sullivan, A. P. Willits Elementary School (NY), Kindergarten
Annie Thoms, Stuyvesant High School (NY), 9th–12th grades
Anthony Tumolo, Readington Township Public Schools (NJ), Kindergarten–8th grades
Janice Wilke, The Baldwin School (PA), 9th–12th grades
Lorin Wilson, Parkside Intermediate School (CA), 6th–8th grades

Thank you to The College of New Jersey's (TCNJ) School of Education for funding the grant that helped us write this book. Our smart and driven colleagues and friends at TCNJ made this work possible. We are grateful for such a supportive work environment.

Thank you to Druscilla Kojiem, Kerry Rushnak, Joely Tores, and Sreenidhi Viswanathan, our research assistants extraordinaire! Your insight, organization, and passion made our writing process smooth and focused, and your research and social media brilliance have helped bring the Toolbox community come to life! These qualities are part of the many gifts you will share with your future students!

Thank you to Nelly Sanchez Aranda, the brilliant artist who inspired the logo for our series and beautifully crafted this book's cover. A special shout out to Zola for inspiring (and requiring) the pink on the cover, which Nelly integrated so well.

Thank you to the teachers and students who inspired this book! We are humbled by your commitment to teaching and learning, and we hope this book serves as a solid resource for you.

Last, but not least, thank you to our families. Andrew, Anna, and Ben, Maureen appreciates your patience, support, and constant inspiration! Becca, Zola, and Kai, Jonathan is grateful for your unwavering love and support that inspired this book and so much more. We are excited to see how this book can impact and influence Zola, Kai, Ben, and Anna's future teachers!

Introduction

WELCOME

Thank you for reading the second book in our *Building Your Teaching Toolbox* series. In this book, we focus specifically on classroom climate. Whether you are a new teacher, veteran teacher, or somewhere in between, you have probably put a lot of thought and effort into creating a classroom environment that is safe, supportive, brave, and engaging. In this book, you will learn how practicing teachers in diverse school and classroom contexts have implemented successful strategies to create and maintain a positive classroom climate that enables *all* students to thrive.

WHO WE ARE

As authors and teachers, we represent varied educational settings. We work together as professors of education at The College of New Jersey (TCNJ), which is where we met. We also are part of the CBK Associates team of consultants working with Youth Leadership Councils in New York City and with educators all over the world.

Jonathan's teaching career began as a social studies teacher at Lloyd Memorial High School, a low-income, public high school in northern Kentucky, where he taught for three years. He then moved to teach in New York City for four years in two separate, Title I, public schools: Urban Assembly School of Design and Construction (Manhattan high school) and Eagle Academy for Young Men at Ocean Hill (Brooklyn 6–12 school). Jonathan taught Global History, New York State Regents and Advanced Placement (AP) US History, Government, Economics, and a course on Race in America. Jonathan was also an adjunct professor for four years at John Jay College, Hunter College, and Brooklyn College, where he taught courses in education, pedagogy, and sociology. During his more than a decade of teaching before becoming a professor of education, Jonathan served as a department chair, instructional coach, and field supervisor for student teachers. At TCNJ, where he coordinates the Urban Secondary Education Program, he focuses his research and practice on culturally responsive and sustaining pedagogy—specifically on how to adapt strategies to support the needs of all types of learners in all types of settings. Jonathan recently published his book *Classroom Management in Teacher Education Programs* (Palgrave Macmillan).

Maureen taught English for 15 years at Mineola High School, a public high school in a middle-class, suburban town on Long Island, New York. There she taught general education and inclusion English classes, literacy support, and AP Language and Composition. The range in abilities among her students made her realize the importance of sharing and gathering strong and successful lesson ideas with colleagues. Maureen was also the coordinator for Service Learning for the New York Metropolitan area and worked at Queens College, Molloy College, and Adelphi University as an adjunct professor of education. She has provided professional development (PD) focused on service learning and literacy across the US and in several other countries. Maureen has published three books: *Getting to the Core of English Language Arts, Grades 6–12* (Corwin); *Getting to the Core of Literacy for History/Social Studies, Science, and Technical Subjects, Grades 6–12* (Corwin); and *Next Generation Literacy: Using the Tests (You Think) You Hate to Help the Students You Love* (ASCD). Maureen's research and practice is focused on practical strategies and planning that support students' application of knowledge and skills to issues that matter to them.

As teacher educators and consultants, our passion, teaching, and research is focused on practical, pedagogical methods to support the needs of preservice and in-service teachers.

WHY WE WROTE THIS BOOK

We wrote this book as schools began reopening after months of virtual learning due to the coronavirus disease 2019 (COVID-19) pandemic. Teachers were serving as the models for K–12 students for how to create a positive social and learning environment in classrooms that felt both familiar and unfamiliar at the same time.

In the preface to his book, *Between Teacher and Child*, Haim Ginott (1972) described the importance of the teacher in modeling and setting the tone for students:

> I have come to the frightening conclusion that I am the decisive element in the room. It is my personal approach that creates the climate. It is my daily mood that makes the weather. . . . In all situations it is my response that decides whether a crisis will be escalated or de-escalated and a child humanized or dehumanized. (15)

Ginott's words remind us that it is important for the teacher to model self-regulation, openness, connection, and progress rather than serving as a disciplinarian.

Too often, teachers think that classroom management should be rooted in discipline, control, and order (Bear, 2015; McLaughlin & Bryan, 2003; Rist, 1972). Such an approach to classroom management embodies a deficit mindset that highlights what students are not doing and supposedly cannot do (Gutstein et al., 1997; Weiner, 2003, 2006) rather than focusing on students' assets (Boykin & Noguera, 2011; Cartledge et al., 2015; Gutiérrez & Rogoff, 2003; Weiner, 2003). As teachers and teacher educators, we have worked to shift the dialogue regarding classroom management from centering on a reactive approach focused on maintaining control to a proactive approach focused on creating an engaging, positive, classroom learning environment. We wrote this book to provide you with accessible tools that can help you use this proactive approach to create and maintain your optimal classroom climate.

KEY CONCEPTS TO CONSIDER

Maslow before You Can Bloom

When we first heard the quote, "You gotta Maslow before you can Bloom," from Dwayne Reed (2019) at the ASCD Empower 19 Conference in Chicago, something just clicked for both of us. We had studied Maslow's (1943) hierarchy of needs and Bloom's Taxonomy (1956) but had never seen how they relate to one another in this way. It turns out the quote has been used for more than a decade by educators like Tomaz Lasic (2009), Jeff Duncan-Andrade (2011), and Jake Miller (2016) to emphasize that teachers must help students meet their physiological and safety needs before they can achieve love and belonging, esteem, and self-actualization. Only then, can students truly embark on Bloom's Taxonomy where they start by building a foundation of knowledge and move toward higher-level application, analysis, synthesis, and evaluation.

Social Emotional Learning

When we work with students to develop a positive classroom climate, we support their social emotional learning (SEL).

> Social and emotional competence is the ability to understand, manage, and express the social and emotional aspects of one's life in ways that enable the successful management of life tasks such as learning, forming relationships, solving everyday problems, and adapting to the complex demands of growth and development. It includes self-awareness, control of impulsivity, working cooperatively, and caring about oneself and others. Social and emotional learning is the process through which children and adults develop the skills, attitudes, and values necessary to acquire social and emotional competence. (Elias et al., 1997, p. 2)

By creating and maintaining a classroom climate that is safe, brave, and welcoming to all students, we model SEL and nourish it.

Dynamic Classroom Management Approach

The Dynamic Classroom Management Approach (DCMA) was created to get teachers to re-envision what classroom management means and focus on creating positive classroom learning environments. DCMA is broken into four domains: Flexibility, Diversity, Pedagogy, and Classroom Culture and Community (Davis, 2017), which collectively help teachers engage their students and create optimal learning environments where each student feels supported, challenged, and seen. For DCMA to work optimally, teachers must think critically about how they can best create positive classroom learning environments and adapt those strategies to meet the needs of each student they teach.

Culturally Responsive/Sustaining Teaching

The strategies in this book are grounded in culturally responsive and sustaining teaching practices that embrace the theory of culturally relevant pedagogy (CRP) developed by Ladson-Billings (1995) and the movement toward Geneva Gay's (2010) culturally relevant teaching, which focused on the practical application of CRP, "using the cultural knowledge, prior experiences, frames of reference, and performance styles of ethnically diverse students to make learning encounters more relevant to and effective for them" (31). Scholars such as Villegas and Lucas (2002), Weinstein et al. (2004), and Paris and Alim (2017) extended the application of culturally relevant teaching to be integrated into classroom management and more sustaining practices. A focus on culturally relevant teaching is critical because teachers can be masters of their content, brilliant lesson designers, and plan the most amazing projects; yet, if they are unable to connect with their students, they will usually not be effective in the classroom.

For this book, we embrace CRP, culturally relevant teaching, and culturally sustaining pedagogy; we use the term culturally responsive/sustaining teaching (CRT) throughout this text as a representation of the synthesis of these approaches. As you read, look for how students are the focus of choices being made in the classroom as well as how they are equal participants in those decisions. Once you are able to support students in taking ownership of their own learning and empowering themselves, you will be able to take academic risks together in the classroom.

HOW THIS BOOK IS ORGANIZED

This book is framed by two overarching questions:

1. What pedagogical strategies have a positive impact on students' learning experiences and the classroom environment?
2. How can we, the researchers, make the intricacies of each pedagogical strategy tangible for novice and experienced teachers working in different settings with varied learners?

For this book, we focus on classroom climate, the foundation for all successful learning. We include strategies related to getting started, routines, and supporting a positive, productive climate.

To make each strategy clear, we detail step-by-step implementation instructions, and to help you envision the strategy further, we provide narratives of the *Strategy in Action*. We also quote teachers explaining why they like each strategy.

Because every teacher's classroom is unique, we give examples of how to modify each strategy based on assets and needs of the classroom context, such as technology, cultural diversity, and available time. We also suggest ways to adapt the strategy based on grade level (elementary, middle, high). To help you consider ways to modify the strategy for English-language learners, Special Education, and Gifted and Talented students, we created a table with frequent modifications that we mark with an *X* if applicable to the strategy described.

As you read through strategy descriptions and professional anecdotes and commentary, we hope you feel like a part of a larger community of educators who are eager to share and grow together.

But wait, there's more! In addition to the 20 strategies described in the initial chapters of this book, we include a list of 10 simpler to implement bonus strategies. We describe these strategies as being a light lift on your part with a heavy impact for your students.

WHY THIS BOOK IS FOR *ALL* TEACHERS

Our work with teachers spans multiple states and countries and connects us with varied school environments. We decided to capitalize on this diversity by developing a book that will help increase the tools teachers can use with their students and help teachers to make mindful decisions about when and how to use those tools based on their students' learning needs.

Research shows that teacher preparation must help preservice teachers develop an array of strategies *and* the ability to reflect on each strategy according to their given setting to plan on how best to proceed (Darling-Hammond, 2015). We believe that this is good practice for *all* educators, regardless of where they are in their careers. This book is intended both to introduce teacher candidates and novice teachers to new strategies and to provide support for the growth and reflective practice of more seasoned teachers.

OUR CONTRIBUTORS

We are incredibly grateful to the 30 teachers who contributed to this book. We were fortunate to gather information from educators across 14 states (Arizona, California, Connecticut, Florida, Missouri, North Dakota, Nebraska, New Jersey, New York, Pennsylvania, Oregon, Texas, Virginia, Wyoming) and three countries (France, Kuwait, US). Our contributors represent a balance of urban (10 teachers), suburban (14 teachers), and rural (6 teachers) settings as well as a range of experience in elementary, middle, and high school; many of the teachers have also taught in multiple settings during their career.

In preparation for the interview process, we asked each contributor to share information regarding their school setting. In the table that follows, we list the percentage of contributors who chose each descriptor as a match for their school. In some categories, you will note that the number of contributors does not equal 30. This is because some contributors believed their school to fall somewhere in the middle of the descriptors. You can see there is a wide range of assets and needs in the schools that are the "homes" for these teachers, their students, and the strategies within this book.

It was heartening to hear from our contributors that the experience of being interviewed helped them remember and reinforce good strategies. The experience of developing this book reminded us of established approaches or informed us of new approaches to use in our own teaching. For this collaboration and inspiration from teacher contributors, we are more grateful than our words will express.

Contributors' School Contexts: Asssets and Needs

Assets	Percentage (number)	Needs	Percentage (number)
My students don't worry about money for basic needs (food, clothing, etc.).	71% (17 teachers)	My students are distracted by concerns about money for basic needs (food, clothing, etc.).	29% (7 teachers)
My students have access to technology inside and outside the classroom.	93% (26 teachers)	My students do not have access to technology in the classroom or at home.	1% (2 teachers)
My classroom population represents a range of racial and ethnic diversity.	59% (16 teachers)	My classroom community is homogeneous in terms of racial and ethnic diversity.	41% (11 teachers)
My class sizes are small.	39% (9 teachers)	My class sizes are large.	61% (14 teachers)
Students consistently attend school.	82% (23 teachers)	Students do not consistently attend school.	18% (5 teachers)
My day is structured to allow time for individual instruction/feedback.	48% (11 teachers)	I rarely have time for individual instruction/feedback.	52% (12 teachers)
My school provides and makes time for quality professional development.	86% (19 teachers)	I do not have access to quality professional development.	14% (3 teachers)
My school values interdisciplinary learning.	74% (17 teachers)	My school does not value interdisciplinary learning.	26% (6 teachers)
I have strong relationships and consistent contact with my students' parents/guardians.	86% (18 teachers)	I have no relationship or interactions with my students' parents/guardians.	14% (3 teachers)
My students want to learn and see that good grades are a result of their learning.	52% (13 teachers)	My students are more focused on good grades, than actual learning.	48% (12 teachers)

FINAL WORDS

We hope you will be inspired to use the strategies you find in this book. We've structured the strategies in each chapter to be as accessible as possible for teachers from any classroom context through our detailed, step-by-step overviews, teacher narratives, and sample adaptations. Remember, teaching and learning are about trying new ideas and approaches. We want to encourage you to explore new ways to make your classroom an optimal learning environment where you and your students thrive together.

If you have some great stories about how you have used these strategies, please connect with us!

Website: https://buildyourteachingtoolbox.com/
Email: buildyourteachingtoolbox@gmail.com
Twitter: @BuildTeachTool
Instagram: @buildteachingtoolbox
Facebook: Build Your Teaching Toolbox

Chapter 1

Highlights from *Adaptable Teaching*'s Classroom Climate Strategies

Adaptable Teaching: 30 Practical Strategies for All School Contexts (Davis & Connolly, 2022), the first book in the *Building Your Teaching Toolbox* series, includes strategies related to classroom climate, planning, instruction, and professional development. Although *Creating Positive Classroom Climate* focuses exclusively on classroom climate, many of the strategies in this book build on the classroom climate strategies presented in *Adaptable Teaching*. This chapter provides brief descriptions of the classroom climate strategies from *Adaptable Teaching* and steps for implementation.

For the detailed narratives and adaptations for each strategy in this chapter, check out *Adaptable Teaching*!

STRATEGY 1: GROUP AGREEMENTS

Group agreements set norms for interactions and behaviors in the classroom. Based on shared values, teachers and students develop mutually beneficial and acceptable expectations that promote a strong classroom community and a safe space for learning.

Strategy Implementation

To successfully develop lasting group agreements, students and teachers need to recognize that behaviors, whether expected or unexpected, cause other people around them to feel a corresponding way (e.g., calm/happy when you do an *expected* behavior or scared or upset when you do an *unexpected* behavior). With that in mind, consider how your choices and behavior impact the way the classroom environment functions and supports shared values.

1. **Establish the classroom as a community.** A community works together to promote good for all. Help your students see themselves as part of a community by:
   - Creating a visual that represents their classroom community. This visual should include all students' and teacher(s)' names.
   - Discussing how the visual represents important shared values such as:
     - Opportunities to share and to listen
     - Trust
     - Time for independent work
     - Group work
     - Multiple voices in the curriculum

2. **Chart and discuss expected/unexpected behaviors.** Sharing examples of expected and unexpected behaviors helps students visualize positive choices and consider how to respond when they do not follow the agreements.
   - Create a T-chart with *expected* behaviors and *unexpected* behaviors.
   - Share visuals or written examples of different behaviors on cards.
   - Students place the cards in the appropriate category.
   - Discuss the situation described.

3. **Collaborate to develop a list of written agreements.** When developing group agreements, be sure to know *why* you are including each agreement on your list. Reasons for agreements could include safety, time management, empathy, or increased learning. For each agreement:
   - Start by stating *why* the expected behavior is important (e.g., we value all students' voices, so we will stay quiet and attentive when another student is talking and we will share the "microphone" by staying aware of how long we are talking).
   - Discuss each proposed agreement and adapt as needed until the class approves it.
   - Record the decided on agreement (on a large paper, online, or both).

4. **What happens if . . . ?** Before finalizing your group agreements, it is important to consider what could happen if an agreement is not followed. To do this:
   - Go through each agreement, one at a time, to determine implications and next steps for not following the agreement.
   - Make notes next to each agreement that break down the what happens if.

5. **Finalize the group agreements.** After you have added the what happens if, review the group agreements one more time and, if everyone is in agreement, have each person (you included) sign the agreements and post them around the classroom (physically or digitally).

6. **Revisit group agreements.** After some time, review the agreements to ensure they are still relevant. Make changes as needed. If an agreement is not followed, you will need to revisit it. Use these steps:
   - Look at group agreements together to determine which agreement wasn't followed.
   - Consider whether the agreement needs to be revised, and if so, how.
   - Discuss as a class what next steps you can take to support classmates' positive choices as related to the agreement.
   - Create an action plan to promote positive choices and sticking to the agreement.

STRATEGY 2: ESTABLISHING ROUTINES

Establishing routines is a strategy that begins before the first day of school. Teachers start by thinking about their ideal classroom environment and what routines must be established to create that environment. Then, beginning on the first day of school (or before), teachers work collaboratively with their students to review, adapt, and add routines they will practice and maintain throughout the year. Routines can be focused on transitions, instruction, classroom agreements, or any other critical part of the classroom environment.

Strategy Implementation

1. **Determine the classroom environment/culture you want.** Every classroom is unique. Therefore, it is important to think about the classroom environment and culture you want within your classroom. This includes:
   - Tone on entering: Do you want students getting right to work? Do you want time for a check-in?
   - Level of shared teacher-student leadership: Will you determine all next steps or will students have a voice in routines/decisions?
   - Daily structure: Do you want consistency or do you want to mix up the routine?
   - Tone while engaged in learning: Are you OK with chatter as long as students are productive? Are there times when the room should be silent?
   - Closing time together: How do you ensure students are thinking about the learning that took place?

2. **Figure out what routines are necessary to enact your desired environment or culture.** Each part of your desired environment or culture can be created and maintained by developing routines that are easy to understand, engage the students, and develop buy-in by the entire class. Begin by:
   - Jotting down each component of your desired environment/culture. Consider:
     - Physical organization
     - Forms of engagement
     - Daily lesson structure
   - Outlining a plan for how to enact each component. Include how students can practice the routine and how long it will take.

3. **Break down which routines are procedural, organizational, or pedagogical.** To determine the best place and method of integrating each routine into your classroom experience:
   - Categorize your routines. Examples include:
     - *Procedural:* Starting or ending an activity, transitions, lining up, quieting down, hand signals for agreement, questions, or asking for help, leaving the classroom.
     - *Organizational:* Cleaning up stations or supplies, where to turn in work.

- *Pedagogical:* Working with partners or groups, engaging in class discussions, using technology.
- Plan (within your lesson plans) when and how to introduce, model, and practice each routine.

4. **Integrate routines into plans for first days of school.** Make sure you find space in your schedule during the first few days of the school year to integrate and practice each routine. Determine:
   - How many new routines you can realistically and productively introduce each day.
   - The order in which you want to introduce each routine.
   - Where in your lesson you want to integrate each routine.
   - How often you want to reinforce each routine.
   - Which routines you can wait to integrate until after the first week of school.

5. **Discuss, assess, and collaboratively agree on routines with the class.** Although you already determined the routines you would like to integrate into your class, when you would like to integrate them, and how you would like to integrate them, once you meet your class, it is helpful to make them partners in the roll out of each routine. To do this:
   - Be transparent with your students about the overall environment you want to create. Ask students to contribute ideas for how they might add onto or change that overall environment.
   - Brainstorm routines that will support the type of environment the class wants.
   - Discuss each routine and get feedback from the class about: how well it will work, what it will take to consistently work, and if there is anything they would change about it.
   - Record the components of each routine (on paper and digitally if you can) as an anchor that students can reference after the roll out of each routine.
   - Ask students to add routines and go through the same process.

6. **Practice routines.** Based on the order you decided to roll out the routines:
   - Introduce one routine at a time.
   - Practice the routine as many times as needed to ensure students understand and buy into it.
   - Continue to enact the routine daily, practicing it each new day until it becomes second nature for the class.

7. **Reassess routines and adapt as needed.** If you notice a routine is no longer working as you and the class intended, take time to reassess.
   - Engage your class in a Plus/Delta discussion about what is working well with the routine and what you could change to strengthen it.
   - Periodically reassess all routines even if they seem to be working.
   - Consider new routines that would help your class achieve its desired environment.
   - Repeat Steps 5 and 6 for any changed or new routine.

STRATEGY 3: POSITIVE AFFIRMATIONS

Positive affirmations is a strategy designed to recognize the behavioral or academic accomplishments of students either publicly or privately using compliments and gestures, which helps create an environment in which students feel welcomed, appreciated, and respected. Different types of affirmations (e.g., claps, cheers, high fives, chants, etc.) may be taught by the teacher or created by the students themselves. Students who are awarded a positive affirmation may be invited to select their favorite affirmation, making it an especially encouraging acknowledgment. This strategy can support students in taking academic risks because they will feel supported rather than judged.

Strategy Implementation

1. **Greet students at the door.** As students enter your room, greet them with a positive or welcoming tone—small moments for genuine interactions (e.g., "Did you see the game?"; "I love those sneakers"; or "I thought of you when I heard this Drake song."). During this time, you can also direct students to what they should be doing for the start of class. Remember to:
   - Pay attention to each student's affect.
   - Individually address something positive and welcoming about each student before they enter the room.
   - Set the day's expectations for students when they enter the room.

2. **Starting class.** Thank students for being part of the class. If someone comes late, tell them "This class is not complete without you." Let students know the day's expectations for success and reinforce that they are fully capable of accomplishing whatever task or activity you have for them.

3. **Use positive affirmations during whole class or small group instruction.** When engaging in whole class or small group instruction, find multiple ways to give positive affirmations. The goal is to give positive affirmations to each student multiple times per week.

   Teacher-to-Student: When you as the teacher want to *gift* an affirmation to a student or students (either individually or in front of the class), make sure you:
   - Give positive affirmations to a variety of students.
   - Consider what behavior, action, or product you want to affirm.
   - Figure out what kind of positive affirmation you want to give the student.
   - Determine whether the affirmation will be whole class or more subtle.
   - Think about how you are integrating the affirmation(s) into your instruction (stopping instruction or within the flow of instruction).

Whole Class: When the entire class collectively acknowledges something great a student or students have done. The teacher will ask students what kind of cheer they want and then count down "3, 2, 1," then do it together. Think about:
- When the whole class should do an affirmation as opposed to just the teacher.
- Who in the class determines which student gets the whole class affirmation.
- Whether the student being affirmed gets to choose their affirmation or the person who decided to gift the affirmation does so.
- If more than one student should be acknowledged at a time.
- How the affirmations are integrated into the instruction.

Student-to-Student: When students shout out something great one of their peers has done. Consider:
- If students are able to offer affirmations whenever they want during class or only during designated times.
- Whether there is a limit to how many students can offer affirmations at one time.
- When student-to-student affirmations can turn into whole class affirmations.

4. **Using positive affirmations during independent or pair work.** When students are doing independent or pair work, take time to check in on each student and offer affirmations to support their work and spirit. Decide whether:
   - Particular students really need a "pick me up" today.
   - You keep the affirmation between you and the student or pair or open it up to the whole class.

5. **Student choice in affirmation.** If not using teacher-to-student verbal affirmations, consider letting students know you want to give them an affirmation for "X" action and to select how they would like to be positively affirmed for it. Decide when the student:
   - Selects from preexisting class affirmations.
   - Creates their own affirmation.

STRATEGY 4: FAILING FORWARD

Failing forward means looking at mistakes, poor decisions, or not being where we want to be as learners and to grow from what has happened. Students and teachers alike are encouraged to share their shortcomings and recognize that though they may have failed, they themselves are not failures. This approach is highly reflective and grounded in social-emotional learning. It encourages students to recognize their own failures, take pride in them as a part of the learning process, and make decisions about what to do next.

Strategy Implementation

1. **Create a safe, shared environment.** Help students feel comfortable sharing their failures by:
   - Sharing videos or stories of successful people who have failed many times on their path to success.
   - Sharing your own failure with the class.
   - Offering a variety of brain teasers and fail a few times before they find success. You can choose whether to be explicit with students in explaining that they are likely to struggle or fail, or you can let them experience this without forewarning.

2. **Explain/review growth mindset.** Let students know that their brains are wired to improve by:
   - Using a growth mindset self-assessment.
   - Charting results of the self-assessment so students can see where there are commonalities in their responses, and noting that in most cases, people are a mix of fixed and growth mindset.
   - Watching a video or reading an article about growth mindset.
   - Having students develop a list of phrases or ways of thinking that reflect fixed and growth mindsets (e.g., Fixed—"I can't do this"; Growth—"I need to work on my ____ skills to do this.").

3. **Encourage reflection.** Reflection is not judgmental or punitive. This is a time for students to learn from mistakes and be proud of their efforts.
   Possible formats for reflection include:
   - Teacher has a short conference with each student to ask questions and comment on reflections
   - Small group share
   - Full class share
   - Journaling
   - Drawing

   Topics for reflection include:
   - Specific skills to develop to be successful
   - People who may help develop these skills

- Additional knowledge needed
- Where to go to find that information
- Level of motivation to complete the work
- What sparks motivation

STRATEGY 5: CRITICAL FEEDBACK SURVEYS

Critical feedback surveys are focused, digital, or written surveys given to students to elicit feedback on specific learning activities, assessment, or other classroom experiences. Surveys can focus on the students' perceived success of various lesson strategies as well as the overall classroom climate, especially as it relates to each unit. Students are also asked to suggest or create action steps to make improvements to their own learning, an instructional activity, or the classroom environment. Teachers then integrate relevant student feedback into their future planning and practice, demonstrating a commitment to their students' thoughts and needs.

Strategy Implementation

1. **Purpose of the survey.** Teacher or students identify what elements of their units, lessons, activities, or classroom climate they want to critically reflect on and the scope of the intended feedback. Consider the following questions to guide your development of feedback surveys:
   - What elements of the units, lessons, activities, or classroom climate can be strengthened by student feedback?
   - Do you need feedback related to how you implemented your learning experiences, the design of those experiences, or both?
   - Is the feedback for short- or long-term change?

2. **Type of survey.** Based on the determined purpose of your survey, decide the type of survey you want to create to help you and your students meet the intended purpose. Think about:
   Survey mode:
   - Easiest mode of feedback (digital, written, or oral) for your students to complete.
   - Easiest mode of feedback for you and your students to analyze.
   - Technologies that can enhance the survey experience and product (e.g., Google Forms).
   - Mode of feedback that will help students develop critical thinking skills.
   - Varying the mode of critical feedback surveys throughout the year to provide students multiple avenues to critically reflect on their classroom experiences or environment.
   - Time needed to analyze student feedback; digital or written feedback would allow for teachers or students to have more time to examine and analyze feedback.
   - If oral, consider:
     - The best way to ask the survey questions.
     - How you will record student answers.
     - Whether it will be done as a whole class, in small groups, or as a "turn and talk."

Reflective versus action-oriented survey:
- If reflective, develop questions that will help students look back and critically reflect on topics like: where they struggled and excelled, the type of support they need, and how the classroom environment could be improved.
- If action-oriented, develop questions that will help students look forward and critically think about where and how they and their classroom community can grow and move forward.

3. **Survey questions.** Figure out which question types align with your desired survey outcomes.
   - *Open-ended:* Used to elicit detailed, subjective information from students.
   - *Likert:* Used to assess a range of feelings from least to most (e.g., How likely are you to use a graphic organizer like this again? Not likely, Somewhat likely, Very likely).
   - *Multiple choice or rankings:* Used when you want students to highlight or order their beliefs around a particular question.
   - *Select all that apply:* Used to give students choices to provide feedback within a contained number of selections.

4. **Time allocation for survey.** Determine how much time is needed for students to complete the survey and when you can allocate that amount of time during class. Below are possible times you might want to have students complete the surveys:
   - Do informal check-ins with students after any learning experience to gauge their thoughts.
   - Have students complete exit tickets at the end of the lesson that ask them to critically reflect on particular elements of the day.
   - Give students a summative critical feedback survey at the conclusion of a project or unit.
   - Have students fill out a survey at the end of your marking period (or year).

5. **Analyze student feedback.** Analyze and make meaning of the feedback to prepare for your student debrief and begin to consider ways to implement the suggestions. Decide:
   - The best way to analyze the student feedback (e.g., take notes, make a list, write questions, etc.).
   - How you will make meaning of the student feedback.
   - How to debrief your analysis of the student feedback with your students.

6. **Debrief feedback with students.** Find the best time during your class period to debrief the feedback with your students. Ensure you allocate enough time so students feel heard and the debrief is collaborative rather than teacher-centered. To do this, consider:
   - The best time to have the debrief with the students (i.e., directly after receiving the feedback or at a later time).
   - How the discussion can be structured to support student voice.

- How you will respond to student suggestions to ensure students feel heard.
- Being transparent about how you plan to integrate their feedback (or not).
- Preparing to have *tough conversations* with students about issues raised from the survey.

7. **Integrate feedback into your teaching.** Try out the students' suggestions and be transparent about how and when you are implementing them.

8. **Reflect on integration of feedback.** Do your own critical reflection on the new changes and consider getting another round of student feedback on the effectiveness of the changes.

Chapter 2

Getting Started

In this chapter you will find strategies for establishing a positive classroom climate with your students at the start of the school year. These include:

- Creating a **Room Setup** that is inviting and practical (Strategy 6).

    Classroom design can do a lot for class morale and climate.

    —*Allison Snyder*, chapter contributor

- **Getting to Know Students** (Strategy 7) and using what you know in your teaching.

    You can't ask them to learn with you unless you're willing to acknowledge them as the individuals they are.

    —*Ann Neary*, chapter contributor

- Using **Team-Building Games** to build community (Strategy 8).

    I like this strategy because everyone is participating and active. In addition, it allows for learning from peers in different, game-like formats.

    —*Mindy Resnick*, chapter contributor

HIGHLIGHTS

- Check out options for flexible seating and how to introduce these choices to students in **Room Setup** (Strategy 6).
- Explore ways to integrate what you learn about students into your curriculum in **Getting to Know Students** (Strategy 7).
- Learn about how to reconnect after breaks with Fall Break Madness or Sadness in **Team-Building Games** (Strategy 8).

GUIDING QUESTIONS

As you read through this chapter, consider the following:

1. How does my classroom setup enhance students' learning and social experiences?
2. In what ways do students see themselves reflected or represented in our classroom space?
3. How can I connect with students in my classroom?
4. How can I connect with students outside my classroom?
5. In what ways can I develop and reinforce connection and collaboration among my students?

STRATEGY 6: ROOM SETUP

> Teacher Contributors
> *Larissa McElrath, Millstone River Elementary School (NJ), 4th grade*
> *Allison Snyder, Bernards High School (NJ), 9th–12th grades*

Room setup is more than just making the classroom look pretty. It's about communicating a message to students that their work and their voices will be prominent; they will be able to find readings and materials that connect with their interests; and they will have options for creating optimal working conditions.

Strategy Implementation

1. **Determine display space.** It is helpful to have designated spaces for: charts, student work, your class calendar, class announcements, the day's agenda, or classroom jobs. When deciding the ideal display spaces, consider visibility and accessibility.

2. **Configure furniture.** Depending on the furniture in the room and the mobility of that furniture, you have several decisions to make.
   - *Students' Desks:* Based on whether you have desks or tables, and the size and shape of the room, think about the optimal way to organize students' desks:
     - Rows may make it easy to walk around the room and monitor student work.
     - Grouped into tables will support cooperative learning.
     - U-shape or rows facing each other will encourage discussion since students can see one another.
   - *Teacher Desk or Podium:* The placement of your teacher desk or podium should be practical and functional. Because you want to move all over the room and have a designated spot to return to when getting students' attention, or sharing important information, think about its ideal location. Ask yourself:
     - Is that space convenient for writing on the board and making eye contact with all students?
     - Do I have ample space (i.e., will I be able to avoid tripping over things)?
   - *Supplies/Materials:* Create designated spaces for classroom supplies like markers or scissors. Have a bin or set of hanging folders where students drop off their work and set up pickup spaces for handouts. That way, if a student is absent, they know where to go to find the materials they missed.

> Allison Snyder created a Take What You Need set of drawers filled with pens, masks, feminine products, aromatherapy, and even positive affirmations. Her students love being able to inconspicuously get supplies from this spot. (See *Sample Materials* on page 27.)

3. **Classroom library.** If you have a classroom library, develop an organizational system that works for you and your students. With any luck, that library will grow each year, so you will benefit from having a good system in place. Some ways to organize your library include:
   - Organize by genre and author's last name.
   - Indicate reading level.
   - Know where your "heavy hitters" (your most popular books) are, so you can easily share.
   - Make a *Students' Favorites* display.
   - Showcase what you are reading.
   - Create a checkout and return process.

> I know where all my heavy hitters are. When there is something I know a student is going through, I will grab a book off the shelf and share it with them. It's a way of saying, "I see you. I see what you're going through, and here's something that I think will help you."
>
> —*Allison Snyder*

Tips for Building a Classroom Library*

- Go to library sales.
- Check out publishing warehouse sales.
- Post requests on community websites and listservs.
- Start a GoFundMe.
- Find nonprofits who donate books like: https://www.booksmiles.org.
- Ask students to donate books they can part with or money to purchase books if they have the means.

*Many of these tips are good for gathering general classroom supplies too!

---

4. **Flexible seating.** Providing choice with seating is about more than just comfort. It can increase student engagement, set a positive tone, give students opportunities to practice taking turns and in making responsible choices, and so much more. To implement flexible seating:
   - *Present All of the Options:* Describe all of the types of seating, and be sure to explain the benefits and possible distractions for each choice.
   - *Explain the System for Signing Up:* Keep things organized with a sign-up system that works for you and your students. Be sure to:

Flexible Seating Options

• Wobble stools	• Bean bag chairs	• Yoga mats
• Couch	• Cushions	• Benches
• Adirondack chairs	• Bungee chairs	
• Yoga balls	• Stools	

- Avoid first come-first serve because it becomes unfair for students whose buses arrive later or who are coming from a class that is far away.
- Create a rotating schedule of groups of four or five students, so each group gets first pick once a week.

- *Model How to Select a Seating Option:* Bring the system to life by modeling how to use it. For example:
  - Move a magnet with your name to your seating option on the board.
  - Add your name to a sign-up list.

> Some kids don't want to move. Some need it. Yoga balls and wobble chairs are great for controlled movement.
> —Larissa McElrath

- *Model and Agree on Norms for Flexible Seating*:
  - Discuss what is appropriate and what is distracting.
  - Model sitting, and ask for feedback on how well you are using your chosen type of seat. Get dramatic with it! Ask students to consider:
    - Do I look comfortable?
    - Do I look focused?
    - Might I distract others by the way I'm sitting?
  - Model transitioning between the base seat and flexible seating option.
  - Post lists of expectations on desks or in areas where there are flexible seating options.

> So much of what I do is me using myself as a model. The more you SHOW and model expectations, the better!
> —Larissa McElrath

- *Check-In:* After using flexible seating for one to two weeks, ask what is working and whether any changes need to be made to seating locations, options, the sign-up system, etc.

5. **Show who you are.** If your space feels like home to you, it is more likely to feel like home to your students. Add touches that reflect who you are. If you are a gardener, bring in plants. Love crafts? Bring in some of your do-it-yourself projects. If you're a sports fan, hang up some swag from your favorite team. This will open up conversation and connection with students.

6. **Create spaces for students to leave their mark.** Students want to see themselves reflected in their space. This can mean posting student work, of course, but it can go much further. Work together to display some or all of the following:
   - Class photos
   - Photos of students with friends, family, pets, etc.
   - A graffiti wall or quote wall where students can post ideas that matter to them
   - For older students, create a selfie wall that connects to your content area.
   - Students' signatures on a piece of furniture, a photo matting, or any other place of choice. Students come back year after year and are excited to see their mark remains!

Considering Different Types of Learners

Though each of the adaptations are likely to benefit all students, the "X" marks indicate adaptations to this strategy that are particularly helpful for English-language learners, Special Education students, and Gifted and Talented students.

English-Language Learners				
Provide visuals	Label materials in multiple languages	Translate instructions/ materials to their primary language	Model expectations/ processes	Invite students to write/speak in primary language
X	X		X	
Special Education Students				
Scaffold instructions/ chunking	Provide positive reinforcement	Schedule breaks	Offer multiple options/formats for student to choose	Minimize distractions
X	X			X
Gifted and Talented Students				
Encourage students to focus on learning rather than grades	Celebrate nonacademic successes with students	Provide opportunities for students to take individualized ownership of learning	Challenge students to use more sophisticated vocabulary	Invite students to share how their thinking is extended by hearing new perspectives
X	X			

WHY I LIKE THIS STRATEGY

Classroom design can do a lot for class morale and climate. Designing a classroom setup that is bright, colorful, and welcoming can immediately set a positive tone. Because of the consistent display of student work and a robust classroom library, my students know how much I value their input and my subject area simply by walking into my room. They know they are in a space that feels like home to me, so they are more inclined to be at home as well.

—*Allison Snyder*

I specifically like using flexible seating because of all the research-based positive benefits.

—*Larissa McElrath*

How to Implement the Strategy at Varied Grade Levels

Elementary	Middle	High
*Place important supplies and sign-up spaces at heights that are easy to see and reach. *Create classroom jobs for students to help with classroom maintenance like setting up the sign-up pages for flexible seating. (See Strategy 9: Classroom Jobs.)	*Encourage students to contribute to the classroom design by suggesting themes or ideas for displays or furniture setup. *Build on classroom jobs by asking students to help with the classroom library or flexible seating maintenance.	*Embrace students' interests and talents. If a student is crafty, give them the opportunity to design part of the space. If they are interested in psychology, ask them to propose a design that takes into consideration the impact of color on mood, etc. *Connect the classroom design with dorm room or office space design.

STRATEGY IN ACTION: TAKE THE STAGE

In my room, I talk a lot about soft skills. Eye contact, shaking hands, being able to talk to others. This led me to thinking about getting a stage. When you're on stage, you have to be able to be heard, stand confidently, make eye contact. My dad built a stage for my classroom.

It was amazing to see the impact this had on students. When they were sharing their ideas, they would jump on stage. I was able to tell them "You're stepping on the stage. This is a big deal! All eyes are on you!"

Not every student wants to jump on stage and that is OK. I always have my students stand to speak and give the option of staying where they are or hopping on stage. I let them know, "Your voice is so important that you get to stand and wait until you have everyone's attention to speak."

Sadly, I had to deconstruct our stage after a Fire Marshall visit. Students clearly missed this element of our classroom, so I rethought how to make it work, and I improvised by adding a low table for students to stand on.

It was important to bring back the stage. Though I provide choice, most kids prefer to share from the stage. They know that their contributions matter in our classroom, and the stage literally and figuratively elevates their voices.

—*Larissa McElrath*

Adaptation for Different Assets and Needs

Funding	
Limited Funding *Build your space little by little. Bring in new elements each school year. Ask colleagues and community members for donations. *Ask students to bring in something that brings them comfort. It may not be a special seat, but it can give the security that will enable them to focus.	***Lots of Funding*** *Poll students to see what types of seating or organizational supplies will be most effective. Ask them to help you with budgeting based on what you find out. *Sponsor a partner classroom. Gather supplies and donate to a teacher and students who want to make their space extra special.
Time	
Limited Time *Make a list of the setup elements you want to take care of in order of priority. Start with the most important and consider where you can ask for student volunteers to help. *Make room setup day a party for you and your colleagues. Work together to get each of your rooms looking great, and then grab some lunch to celebrate!	***Lots of Time*** *Take a day to step back and assess how your room is working for you and your students. What organizational elements could use an upgrade? Use your extra time to take action on these! *Give students even more opportunity to leave their mark on the classroom. Invite them to design and create spaces within the room or rearrange existing spaces in ways that work best for them.

STRATEGY IN ACTION: STUDENTS LEAVE THEIR MARK

I always love the first day of school because I get to see my new students' initial reactions to my classroom. Thousands of books line the walls. A blank "Reading Graffiti" bulletin board surrounded by twinkling lights awaits their contributions. A desk covered with student signatures sits at the front of the room. A comfy "Book Nook" beckons for them to sit. This is a space that has been designed with love, and students know it. Before a "hello," I am often met with a smile and an audible "whoa!"

On one first day a few years ago, my "Reading Graffiti" bulletin board must have beckoned Sean. He was a soft-spoken freshman who lingered after class, sweetly asking me if he could be the very first to "tag" my board. He had a quote from, *Moneyball*, his summer reading book, all picked out: "The pleasure of rooting for Goliath is that you can expect to win. The pleasure of rooting for David is that, while you don't know what to expect you stand at least a chance of being inspired." Posting this quote on the first day gave this quiet student a way to find his place in our shared space.

Students know my room is as much theirs as it is mine. I so often see students wanting to leave their mark. Some write "Reading Graffiti." Some give me their school portraits for me to hang on my "mug shot" corkboard. Some sign my desk. Some give me college pennants as seniors. And some, like Aoife, paint me stunning scenes from the novels we read that I will proudly frame and display on my classroom walls for life.

—*Allison Snyder*

Sample Materials

Photos of Allison Snyder's Classroom Setup
Allison Snyder

STRATEGY 7: GETTING TO KNOW STUDENTS

> Teacher Contributors
> *Brenda Bokenyi, César Chávez Elementary School (OR), 1st grade*
> *Ann Neary, Staples High School (CT), 10th–12th grades*

Getting to know students creates the foundation for developing a strong and positive classroom community. Learning about your students begins on or before the first day of school, both inside and outside the classroom. Use the information you learn about students' background, assets, and needs to develop curriculum, units, lessons, and activities that are meaningful to students and make their learning come alive.

> You're making a big ask of students because you're asking them to follow you with whatever you're teaching. They won't want to follow you and the other students if they don't feel comfortable in the environment. They want someone who cares about them and treats them like people. You can't ask them to learn with you unless you're willing to acknowledge them as the individuals they are.
>
> —*Ann Neary*

Strategy Implementation

How you get to know your students will depend on the context of your school community and what you are able to manage as the teacher. It is important to get to know your students both inside and outside of the classroom and then find ways to integrate that knowledge into your teaching.

Part I: Getting to Know Students and Their Families Outside School—Home Visits and Extracurriculars

1. **Contact families and schedule home visits.** Reach out to families to schedule a home visit that will help you start building relationships with students and their families. When communicating, consider:
   - *When:* Once you receive your finalized class list before the school year starts, gather your students' contact information and reach out to their families immediately.
   - *How:* You can reach out to families by email, phone, or mail. If you have access to all three means of communication, start by sending an email. If you do not get a response, call their home. If you cannot reach them by phone, send a letter in the mail. All of these forms of communication should be done in the students' home language.
     - NOTE: After two or three attempts to contact a family using multiple methods without a response, respect the family's decision to not do a visit. Yet, continue to communicate with the family to celebrate their child and let them know about important classroom and school events, even if they never respond to you.

> **Don't Speak the Language? Find Ways to Connect!**
>
> - Use translated materials.
>   - You can use websites like www.wordreference.com or Google Translate to help with translation.
>   - Have all materials reviewed by a native speaker.
> - During the visit, consider:
>   - Having the student, if they are comfortable, act as a translator between you and the family.
>   - Bringing a colleague with you that speaks the home language of the family.

- *What to Include:* Convey to the families that the purpose of the visit is casual and to get to know them and their child. Give families the choice of scheduling a visit before school starts or after it begins.
- *Time:* Schedule the visits for 30 minutes, which is enough time to have meaningful conversations, but it is also short enough where it does not feel like a burden on the families. Additionally, scheduling blocks of time for back-to-back visits with ample travel time in-between allows you to meet with several families in a shorter amount of time.
- *Prioritizing Some Students:* Connect with your students' teacher(s) from the previous year to see if there are particular students or families who would benefit from an early home visit. Prioritize early visits with those students as well as students who are missing contact information because this might be a signal that the student and their family need strong connections with the school community.
- *Goal:* Visit more than half of your students' homes before the first day of school. Most families prefer these early visits and once the school year begins, it is harder to make time for the visits after the school day.

2. **Prepare for the home visit.** It's good to be transparent with families about how they can prepare for the visit and gather all the materials you will need before starting your first visit.
    - *Families:* Let families know that they will dictate the nature and tone of the visit. Tell them to think about sharing anything they would like for you to see or experience.

> **Why Home Visits?**
>
> - Get to know students in their home context and without others around.
> - Conversations can be personal.
> - Make connections and start relationship building with your students' families.
> - Help your students and their families feel prepared and comfortable about becoming part of your classroom community.

- *Teacher:* Prepare your classroom handbook (or its equivalent) to give to families that lets them know important information about your classroom and curriculum. Also, gather games or books that might be of interest to your students or members of their family.

3. **Conduct the home visit.** It is important to follow the lead of the family. Some families have questions they want to ask. Some students want to show you their whole home, whereas others want to sit in the living room and talk more formally. And some families might not be comfortable with a home visit, for many reasons, so offer an option like a phone or Zoom call.
    - Give the family your classroom handbook and go over it so they get a sense of your classroom community and structure. If doing the visit remotely, you can mail or email the classroom handbook to the family.
        - NOTE: If you have not met with a family by the first day of school, give your student the handbook to take home so they have answers to commonly asked questions that you can then discuss when you conduct your visit.
    - If families are not sure what to do:
        - Ask the student, "Is there anything you want to show me?"
            - Let the student take you anywhere in the home where they feel comfortable and show you anything that interests them.
        - Ask the parent or guardian, "Anything you want to know about my classroom, the school, or the school community?"
            - Be prepared to ask guiding questions that provide context for the school community and class structure that invite follow-up questions.
    - Keep an open mind:
        - If the family shares something that is new or seems strange to you, ask questions to learn more rather than showing any signs of disapproval.
        - Enjoy the visit! Families have welcomed you into their home to see their unique culture. This is a personal time to cherish.
    - Take notes on the visit:
        - Stay present and don't focus on your notes during the visit.
        - Let families know you are jotting down notes so you remember small bits of information about the student to best support them in your classroom.
        - Fill in gaps in your notes after leaving the home.

4. **Reflect on the home visits and next steps.** After completing your home visits, take note of all you have learned so you can use that knowledge in your classroom and sustain connections with the students and their families.
    - After *each* home visit, take notes on facts about the student that you need to remember to best support the student and how you can integrate elements of their life and background into your curriculum.
    - After *all* home visits, look at all of your notes and determine similarities and differences among your students, themes that you can integrate into your practice and curriculum, and questions you still need to answer.

- Maintain connections with families once the year starts to touch base, update them about their child, and to continue to learn more about your students. This can be done through emails, classroom newsletters, a class website, phone calls, texts, or platforms like Class Dojo or Remind.

5. **Show up for extracurricular activities.** Whether you are able to conduct home visits or not, a great place to get to know your students and their families is during their extracurricular activities. A few ways to do this include:
    - *Coaching or Advising:* Use your skills to serve as a coach or advisor for a club.
    - *Spectator:* Find out what extracurricular activities your students are doing (have a calendar students can fill out, send out a Google Form, etc.), and show up when you are free! Keep track of who you see and make a concerted effort to try to see as many students as possible in the first few months of the year.
    - *Hallways:* Some students don't engage in extracurricular activities, or maybe you have limited time after school hours. If that is the case, be active in the hallways, connect with students, engage them in conversations not related to school, and just be there for them!

Part II: Getting to Know Students Inside School

1. **Getting ready for Day 1.** Take steps to gather initial information from your students and let them know that on the first day of school they will take time to get to know each other before diving into content.
    - *Pre-Class Survey:* Give students a pre-class survey (e.g., Google Form) that asks students about their: preferred pronouns, background, likes, favorite songs (to create a class playlist), how they learn best, needs in your classroom, etc. The answers to these questions will inform what you decide to include in the Day 1 activity and how you might need to adapt it to be inclusive of your students (e.g., having larger fonts for students with visual impairments).
    - *Pre-Class Prep:* If you plan to have students create and present introductory posters or slides, and you know you won't have enough time in class for students to gather information and materials for these, send a message to your students before the first day of class. Provide them with your poster or slide guiding questions so they have time to think about what they want to include and find images or artifacts they want to use for their slides.

2. **Make it low stakes.** Ensure the initial *getting to know you* activity on the first day of school is accessible and invites all students to participate. To do this:
    - Ask students to answer *safe* questions on their slides or posters that they are likely to be comfortable answering.
    - Let students know to only share anything they are comfortable for everyone in the classroom to see and comment on; what is shared and students' comfort level will vary.

> **Possible Things to Include on "Getting to Know You" Slides or Posters**
>
> - A photo of the student
> - Preferred name and pronouns
> - Words or lyrics of your favorite song, poem, book, or movie
> - Favorite books, hobbies, shows, food
> - Most interesting fact about you
> - Language(s) spoken at home
> - Images that represent your background
> - Pets you have or would like to have
> - Favorite subject at school
> - Family and friends
> - Place you like to visit or dream of visiting

- Do it on Google slides or Jamboard (digitally) or posters that can be placed around the classroom where students can view one another's bios so they can learn together.

3. **Focus on positivity and connection building.** Emphasize the importance of being positive to foster a strong classroom climate.
    - Let students know that when they learn about and comment on one another's slides or posters, to only focus on positive reactions, and when students are confused, to ask questions about clarity and learning more.
    - Explain how important it is that the class knows each other as people and how surprisingly easy it is to find a connection to someone else.

4. **Model with your own slide or poster.** Show the class a model of your own slide or poster that follows the same guidelines and guiding questions you ask students to complete. (See *Sample Materials* on page 38 for models.) Use this slide or poster to:
    - Introduce yourself and talk about each of the elements in your poster or slide.
    - Model how students can create their own slide or poster.
    - Go over how to look at and comment on one another's slides or posters.

5. **Student work time.** Give students time to create their own slides or posters.
    - *Checklist:* Make sure you have a clear checklist of what you want students to include that they can follow as they work.
    - *Check-In:* Determine the amount of time students have for this work, and schedule check-in points to support students and remind them where they should be in the process.
    - *Music:* Consider playing some music in the background (a student-generated playlist if possible!), to set the mood while students work.

6. **Comment on slides or posters.** Once every student has completed their slides or posters, have students comment on at least three other slides or posters. Remind students to focus on the positive and use your model on how to comment before they begin.
   - *Slides:* Ensure all of your students' slides are on the same Google Slides document or Jamboard.
     - Have students quickly read through *all* of the students' slides.
     - Ask students to comment on at least *three other students' slides*.
     - Request that students comment on slides where nobody has commented if they see lots of people commenting on the same slides.

7. **Debrief.** Have students reflect on what they learned about their peers. Ask them to note where they have connections with their peers and what more they want to learn about each other.
   - *Mingle Activity to Discuss Connections:* Give students an opportunity to find and chat with the students where they found the connections or want to learn more.
   - *Full Class Debrief:* Do a quick debrief with the whole class about what they learned, what they liked about the process and the connections they made, and how they can build on this *getting to know you* activity.

8. **Next steps.** Figure out with the class how you can continue to get to know one another. As students get more comfortable, start to integrate deeper questions that can build toward *critical conversations*.

Part III: Integrating Knowledge of Students into Classroom

1. **Connect as people.** Take what you learned about your students from the initial getting to know you experiences to check in with your students. This includes:
   - Asking about their hobbies, family, and other interests.
   - Sending them articles, recipes, or other things that you think your student(s) will find meaningful.

2. **Integrating into the curriculum.** Include connections with students in your planning and your class conversations.
   - *Reevaluate and Adapt Your Curriculum:* Using the information you learned about your students from visits, surveys, or initial getting to know you activities the first week, look at your curriculum to see how you can adapt, change, and enhance it by integrating resources and topics meaningful to your students into your units, lessons, and activities. Examples include:
     - *Writing:* Design writing exercises where students write about something from your home visit or their getting to know you slides or posters.
     - *Intervention Strategies:* Use incentives for students that stem from what you have learned about them.

> **A Family Affair!**
>
> In Brenda Bokenyi's classroom, she has family members come in to celebrate and learn about their traditions and jobs, including:
>
> - A parent who is a map maker (cartographer) came in to share the process.
> - A parent who is an architect came in to look at blueprints with the class.
> - Family members came in to share their family's traditions, including a parent bringing in a traditional mask to explain its significance.
> - A parent brought a traditional math game to play with the students that they donated to the classroom for students to continue to play.

- ○ *Show and Tell (All Ages):* Have students bring in artifacts that celebrate elements of the students and their background or traditions that were highlighted during the home visit or getting to know you activity. Additionally, you can ask families what they do for work and get families to come in to share things about their experiences and expertise and skills.
- *Part of the Learning Dialogue:* Consistently take information you know about your students to use in discussions about your learning (e.g., In an English class, have athletes in the class focus on *training* as a way to learn steps for *close reading*.).

3. **Return to the Slides or Posters and Notes from Home Visit throughout the Year.** Ensure you continually return to the slides or posters or your notes from the home visit to remember little facts about your students. When doing this, add to your notes based on new information you have learned about each student.

4. **Touch Base with Families.** Outside of parent-teacher conferences and back-to-school nights, regularly check in with your students' families to let them know what is going on in your class, great things their child has done, and areas where you are supporting student growth.

Considering Different Types of Learners

Though each of the adaptations are likely to benefit all students, the "X" marks indicate adaptations to this strategy that are particularly helpful for English-language learners, Special Education students, and Gifted and Talented students.

English-Language Learners				
Provide visuals	Label materials in multiple languages	Translate instructions/ materials to their primary language	Model expectations/ processes	Invite students to write/speak in primary language
X		X	X	X
Special Education Students				
Scaffold instructions/ chunking	Provide positive reinforcement	Schedule breaks	Offer multiple options/formats for student to choose	Minimize distractions
X	X			X
Gifted and Talented Students				
Encourage students to focus on learning rather than grades	Celebrate nonacademic successes with students	Provide opportunities for students to take individualized ownership of learning	Challenge students to use more sophisticated vocabulary	Invite students to share how their thinking is extended by hearing new perspectives
X	X			

WHY I LIKE THIS STRATEGY

So many reasons! I get to know families privately without others around. We can have personal conversations. I get to see students in their own environment in a positive light. If there are issues later on, we have a solid foundation with which to start. During class time I am able to refer back to our visit. For example, if a student is struggling with what to write about, I can talk about their pet, room, or home. Home visits help me build a strong relationship with all families, not just those that are more involved in school and know how systems work. These visits allow me to support families that are not familiar with public school systems in the United States. I can share information with them about how to ask questions, where to go for information, and how to be an advocate for their child.

—*Brenda Bokenyi*

This gives me a great deal of information about my students. It works well for both the quiet ones and the extroverts. It's also a way to hold yourself accountable for *using* the information you ask from students. Same thing with *Google Surveys* you give to students. You then need to match what you learn with the person—make sure you know the information to react to it. And I can use all of this information for activities planned for learning throughout the year.

—*Ann Neary*

How to Implement the Strategy at Varied Grade Levels

Elementary	Middle	High
*Make the questions accessible to students so they can respond verbally, artistically, or in writing. *Choose a reasonable number of *getting to know you* questions based on your students' ages.	*Make the questions accessible to students and challenge them to respond verbally, artistically, *and* in writing. *Try to attend extracurricular events students are part of and interact with families there.	*Push students to explore different parts of their background and identity verbally, artistically, or in writing. *Show students that you are noticing their interests and skills by encouraging them to join extracurricular activities that fit with their home and possible working obligations. This is a great way for students to enhance their college applications and develop transferable skills.

STRATEGY IN ACTION: THE VALUE OF HOME VISITS

I first started doing home visits when I taught Pre-K in Aurora, Illinois. They were built in as part of the program. We taught Monday through Thursday and did visits on Fridays. I visited each of my 40 students (20 AM and 20 PM) two or three times during the year. These visits with a high poverty population were more structured with a purpose to provide families with information about how to support their child's education at home.

I took the practice of home visits with me when I moved to Portland, Oregon. I was not able to start the visits again until I returned to the same school for a second year. I needed to have that consistency and time before the school year began to do home visits again.

In my 13 years of teaching in Portland I have done hundreds of visits with all types of families. I have had cookies baked for me, grandparents invited over, tours of gardens, a visit in a family restaurant, and many conversations in small living rooms. By meeting families in their own space, I have had open, honest conversations. One family shared that they were having safety issues with their landlord and needed help. Many have had lists of questions they want to ask that they never have time to ask at school. I have had families share about divorce, death of a parent, and special needs of their child. This is information that I may never hear in the course of a regular school year, but I hear it at home visits. These conversations are invaluable.

—*Brenda Bokenyi*

Adaptation for Different Assets and Needs

Time	
Limited Time	**Lots of Time**
Home Visits. Try to get as many visits in before school starts and be very strict about keeping each visit to 30 minutes or less.	*Home Visits*. Try to schedule follow-up home visits to retain and build on your connection with families.
Slides and Posters. Have a clear checklist for what students need to produce and have them come to class with all the resources they need to finalize the slides and posters in class.	*Slides and Posters*. Use more class time to develop and comment on slides and posters.

Student Personality	
Reserved	**Open**
In-Class Sharing. Let quieter students see others share before you call on them so they will know what to expect from you and their peers.	*In-Class Sharing*. Call on these students to be models for sharing. Help them recognize when it is time to give others time to share.
Connecting Outside of Class. Start by consistently checking in with these students in the hallways, and once they share extracurriculars they are part of, show up, give them praise, and follow up when you see them the next day.	*Encourage students to invite more reserved students into dialogue about their lives.

STRATEGY IN ACTION: GETTING TO KNOW YOU SLIDES

While I used this effectively in all my English Language Arts classes, I found it especially effective in my AP Lit class and my World Lit class. AP Lit tends to have students who are academically competitive, worry about someone being smarter than they are or more competent. Because of those fears they tend to keep others at bay and that is counterproductive to the community spirit I seek. What I found with this activity was, they were willing to share, became more invested in each other, and made connections they did not expect. Who knew I'd have four vegans in one class and they would share food websites?

It works because you're not saying Day 1, "let's read the syllabus." You don't take attendance or do roll call. Instead, you start talking to the students and learn about names and pronouns, which are also on the Google Survey. It sets the tone that "we're going to be OK in this class."

At the other end of the academic spectrum are my World Lit students who tend not to be as motivated academically, but also worry about their own intellect and are shy about speaking up. This format allows them to reveal themselves in a rather non-threatening way and form bonds they may not have created.

The big takeaway is this works across the board for all students and lets me know a lot about them as we begin a semester together.

—*Ann Neary*

Sample Materials

Birthdate: September 9 !!!!

Members of my family: 8 (6 kids!!!!)

Things I like to do when I'm not at school: ride Finbar, sail, work in the forest, bake (and eat)

Biggest pet peeve: people being unkind

Three words that describes me: hopetimistic, happy, curious

One thing everyone should know about me: I am interested in **your** story

One thing people usually get wrong about me: I am funny!!! Really. I am!

I could eat this food item every day of my life: apples, especially Pink Ladies

Favorite YouTuber (or celebrity in general): Ali Komenova (yoga), Jason Slaughter (not just bikes)

Three things I'm currently (and always) obsessed with: social justice, cooking, teaching

You can ask me about this/these things because I'm kind of an expert: how to find joy in small things, books, outdoor life

Birthdate: Feb 24th

Members of my family: 6 (8 with Pets) - 3 sisters

Things I like to do when I'm not at school: Dance, write for Inklings, cook vegan food, play with my siblings and my dog, watch documentaries, explore new places!

Biggest pet peeve: So oddly specific, but when people say to plus, minus, or times two things together rather than saying add, subtract or multiply

Three words that describes me: Diligent, Thoughtful, Adventurous

One thing everyone should know about me: I love getting to meet and talk to new people!!

One thing people usually get wrong about me: People sometimes think I'm taller than I am - I am very short (5ft to be exact)

I could eat this food item every day of my life: Avocados

Favorite YouTuber (or celebrity in general): Epicurious, specifically the series 4 levels

Three things I'm currently obsessed with: My airfryer, nutcracker music, and France

You can ask me about this/these things because I'm kind of an expert: Animal agriculture's impact on the environment :)

Getting to Know You Slides
Ann Neary

STRATEGY 8: TEAM-BUILDING GAMES

> Teacher Contributors
> Larissa McElrath, Millstone River Elementary (NJ), 4th grade
> Mindy Resnick, Mary Emily Bryan Middle School (MO), 7th–8th grades
> Ryan McCamy, Trenton Central High School (NJ), 10th–12th grades

Team-building games are an important way to build a positive, inviting, and collaborative classroom community. These games, which can start during the first week of school and extend throughout the year, enable students and the teacher to get to know one another in an interactive, fun, and meaningful way that will enhance the classroom learning environment.

Strategy Implementation

Some games are ideal to use at the start of the year because they help you and your students learn each other's names and learn some basic information about each member of the class. Other games work better further into the school year, when you have a better sense of one another's personalities and want to deepen connections and strengthen teamwork.

Part I: Beginning-of-Year Games

There are numerous games that can be played to help the class get to know one another at the start of the school year. One or more of these games can be played on Day 1 or scattered across the first week or two. Below are games that you can pick and choose from and adapt for your needs follow.

1. **Name games.** A critical element to building a strong classroom community is ensuring everybody knows one another's name. On Day 1, spend time playing a game, like the following, to help everyone learn names:
   - *Animal Association*
     - Have everyone come up with an animal that starts with the same letter as their name.
     - Stand in a circle and have one person at a time say their preferred name and animal, having everyone repeat the new person and every previous person and their animal before moving on to a new person.
     - Once everyone has gone, have somebody stand in the middle of the circle and spin and randomly point at someone, count down from 3, and then have the whole class say the person's name and animal. Repeat as many times as time allows.
     - Lastly, ask for a volunteer who is bad with names to say everyone's name.
   - *Interviewing Peers*
     - Have everyone pair up to chat for four minutes to get to know basic information and fun facts about their partner. Encourage students to take notes.

- Next, ask pairs to introduce one another and their preferred name and pronouns and share a few highlights about their partner.
- After each person is introduced, have the entire class repeat the person's name.
- After each pair goes, go back to all of the individuals who were previously introduced and have the entire class say their names as well as the names of the students in the new pair. (You can switch up the order you review the previous individuals' names to make it more challenging for the class to remember each person's name.) The purpose of this is for students to reinforce their memory of each other's names repeatedly throughout the introductions.
- As with Animal Association, ask for a volunteer who is bad with names to say everyone's name.

> **Teachers, Be PART of the Games!**
>
> Don't just be a facilitator, be a part of the games and get to know the class just like everyone else.

2. **Poker chip races.** This is best done on the first day of classes. It is a series of races that are designed to help the teams learn how to work together to "win." For Poker Chip Races, students sit in rows by team and pass poker chips to one another from front to back, with added layers of clarity and complexity added in with every new race. However, when you start this game, you do not let students know the intention or the desired process. Rather, they have to work together with their teammates to understand what success looks like and how best to collaborate. Students will be confused at first. This is the intention. They will learn to rely on each other for support. This is how the game is played:

   - *Prep:* Create a slideshow for directions for each part of the game (see *Sample Materials* on pages 51–52).

   > Instead of "don't smile until Christmas," smile from Day 1!
   >
   > —*Ryan McCamy*

   - *Introductions:* When students arrive, briefly introduce yourself and go around the room to have students quickly share their preferred name and pronouns.
   - *Agenda:* Post your daily agenda where you typically do and put Races as the main activity, but keep it vague to peak students' curiosity.
   - *Get into Teams and Create a Scorecard:* Randomly break the class into even groups (ideally five students per group) and ask them to create a team name and get ready to race. After teams select their names, create a Scorecard with each team's name and post it on the board.
   - *Start Race 1:* Begin the instructions slideshow with Race 1, hand each group the same number of poker chips and the simple instruction to "GO!" The goal is to be intentionally vague about the goals, expectations, and rules so that pure chaos, confusion, sometimes anger follows as students have no clue what they are doing, how they complete the races, and win. Embrace the chaos and even add to it by pushing them by saying, "GO" or "Let's go; this is a race." Conclude the race when you feel there is a natural ending point and record the "winners" on the scorecard.

- *Follow-Up to Race 1:* After Race 1, get the class settled down and play into the game by asking, "Come on, what's the problem? . . . I was told you were an amazing group of students. . . . That wasn't very impressive."
- *Continue the Races:* Move onto Race 2, Race 3, and so forth. With each race add new instructions, structure, expectations, room for creativity and individualism until they get to the point where they are doing the races with their eyes closed, efficiently and effectively, and even silently. Add to the scorecard after each round. (See *Sample Materials* on pages 51–52.)
- *Debrief the Races:* After the final race, allow students to individually and then collectively debrief the experience. Consider doing it as a think-pair-share, as follows:
  - *Individually:* Have students take a couple of minutes to think about and respond (written, with images, etc.) to guided reflection questions about: (1) What changed from race to race? Why?; (2) How did you achieve success?; (3) How are you defining success?; and (4) How can we implement those same principles of success in our classroom each and every day?
  - *Pairs:* Give students a few minutes to share their reflections with a person sitting next to them; this could be a team member or someone from a different team. Have pairs focus on similarities and differences in their answers.
  - *Share as a Class:* One guiding question at a time, ask pairs to share big ideas that came out of their reflections and discussions. Record answers to each discussion on a Google Slide, the whiteboard, or on poster paper so the class can have these core principles for the class recorded to serve as a framework for classroom agreements (see *Strategy 2: Group Agreements* on pages 9–10 for more information and how to co-create group agreements).
    - NOTE: Use students' debriefs to remind you of elements of their personalities and think about how best to work on team building moving forward.

Reflecting on Poker Chip Races

- *Reflecting on Team Building.* Discuss with students:
  - Different roles in group dynamics.
  - What enables groups to function well.
  - How they can take this experience to improve team dynamics moving forward.
- *Different Personalities.* As the teacher, take note of different personality traits that arise from the races. Consider:
  - Which students are reluctant, and think about how to get them more involved moving forward.
  - Who the vocal students are and how to embrace their voice in an inclusive way.
  - Students that are hyper-competitive and how you might harness that competitiveness in a productive way in your classroom.

> **Strategy in Action: Poker Chip Races**
>
> I wanted to share a rationale for discussing classroom rules, structures, etc. with my high school students, and I wanted a way to make a connection between what we do in our classroom with the larger school, society, workplaces, etc., so I created the Poker Chip Races.
>
> The students respond very well to this strategy and walk out of my room on the first day with smiles on their faces, and I have a smile on my face.
>
> Students typically respond well to the game and are eager to make the connections with lessons learned. The most impacted people by this strategy are often myself, since I get a great feel for the students' personalities, and some of the quieter students who may not want to get involved right away, but are somewhat forced into it for their teams to have success.
>
> The big takeaways from this experience are that it's fun, it builds relationships right away, gives great insight into characteristics of my students, an overall emphasis on why we do things the way we do them in class, and the importance of understanding that rules, expectations, cooperative learning, informed responsible discussion, etc. will play a large role in our success together as a class.
>
> —*Ryan McCamy*

- *Follow-Up Getting to Know You Exercises:* Take time after the debrief (that day or subsequent days) to have students engage in more games and activities where they get to know each other, their different personalities, how they best work together, and just have fun! Connect back to lessons learned from the poker chip game when you debrief.

3. **BINGO.** This is a classic game that can be adapted for any classroom setting.
   - *Pre-Class Survey:* If feasible, have students fill out a pre-class survey before they come to school where you learn fun facts about them.

> **Team-Building Games Help Build Trust Needed for Content and Skill Development!**
>
> Middle School is rough. . . . they do lots of writing and it's hard to share writing in general. To do peer editing and grow your writing you need feedback from your peers and to be able to make mistakes and move forward. Teachers need to create an environment where students are willing to read their writing to their table or the class. I want as many people as possible to be willing to share, and they wouldn't want to do that if they didn't have a community where they trusted people. Team-building games are how I build this community in my classroom. Through team-building games, students develop a trust with one another where they can provide constructive feedback.
>
> —*Mindy Resnick*

- *BINGO Board Creation:* Use facts you learned or know about your students to create a BINGO board that has five rows across and five columns (B, I, N, G, and O).
- *BINGO Rules:* Student must:
  - Talk to one person at a time about one of the boxes that reflects their background or story. Students cannot just ask students, "can you sign this box?," they have to introduce themselves and share a story about it before signing it and then move on to the next person.
  - Use a *different* person for every box.
  - Either get five boxes in a row OR do a *blackout* where they check off each box.
- *BINGO Debrief:* Have students share some of the stories they learned about their peers during the game.

Part II: Check-In Games

In addition to team building games at the start of the year to develop relationships and a strong classroom community, it is critical to create time and space for check-in games to maintain and enhance your classroom community. One example of such a game is *Fall Break Madness or Sadness*, which can be adapted at any point during the school year.

- **Fall Break Madness or Sadness**. Modeled after *March Madness Brackets*, *Fall Break Madness or Sadness* is a game where students compete with one another based on the best and worst things that happened to them during their break.
  - *When to Play:* After any break when students have not seen each other for a while; however, this could be done after a weekend or just a random day that feels right to you.
    - NOTE: Don't play this at the beginning of the year because students need to have already built trust and safety in the classroom.
  - *How to Play:* The game is played as followed:
    - Students journal for five minutes about the best or worst thing from over the break that they are willing to share. They focus on the details of what made their experience the best or worst so they have evidence to support why they feel the way they do about the event. Remind students not to share things their families would not want them to share and to be respectful of boundaries.
    - Place students in groups of four and give them five minutes to share a synopsis of each of their best and worst experiences.

> **Model Sharing for Your Students!**
>
> Before engaging in *Fall Break Madness or Sadness*, Mindy Resnick shares lots of stories about her life, including bad things that happened and why it's OK that happened. This lets students know it's OK to be unhappy, but that there's more in your future. As she tells her students, "You can never really understand someone until you've walked in their shoes."

- *Grouping*: Groups can be sorted in many different ways, randomly or strategically, which might change each time you play.
- *Addressing Differences:* Remind the class that you don't always know what people have been through or experienced and that everyone has different experiences and perspectives. This is important when there is cultural, socio-economic, racial, and other demographic diversity within your classroom.
- *Asset Lens*: As students share, circulate and push them to provide details to support their stories and to focus on the positive whenever possible. You want the experience to be an asset-focused discussion rather than focusing on deficits, something you will need to explicitly model for your students.

○ The group votes on one worst experience and one best experience from their group; one person in the group cannot be selected to represent both the best and worst; each group needs two different representatives.
○ All the BEST go into a bracket for *Fall Break Madness* and the WORST go into a bracket for *Fall Break Sadness*.
○ Vote on whether the class wants to do the BEST or WORST first.
○ Have one student share at a time.
  - Students begin by giving a quick intro/context before they share their story.
  - Ask the class to be attentive and respectful listeners.
  - When really heavy things are shared, take space to talk through it as a class.
○ After each student has shared, the class votes on which one is the "winner."
  - Winners receive a small prize like candy.

STRATEGY IN ACTION: FALL BREAK MADNESS OR SADNESS

Often, when students come back from a break, there have been important shifts in their lives that we need to know about. Sometimes those shifts are positive, and sometimes they are negative. Knowing about what has happened while students have been away from school is so important, so I started playing Fall Break Madness or Sadness to check in with my students. (See description in *Strategy Implementation*.)

Group representatives usually share happy examples first, but I let students decide which bracket they want to begin with. For each topic, the two kids against each other, will read their thing or just say their thing, and then we vote on which one of them moves on to their bracket against each other for the best break and worst break story. For the worst break story, sometimes it will be, "so, and so cheated on me with my best friend and blah blah blah blah,". . . but sometimes it will be, "My dog died, and we had to flush my fish down the toilet and my grandpa got sick," and it's really awful.

The silver lining is that later, the kids will talk with each other about their experiences because, if the student is telling us, it shows that they want to share it with someone.

The winners for each story get their names up on the board for the week, and they get a piece of candy or another small prize.

—Mindy Resnick

- NOTE: After the *Sadness* winner is declared, thank them and the others for sharing and acknowledge that you hope it was a chance to "get it out" and "be acknowledged" for what they went through. DO NOT say, "I totally understand how you feel," because most often, you and the rest of the class will not understand.
  ○ Repeat for the second bracket (*Madness* or *Sadness* depending on which you did first).
- *Follow Up*: Later that day, follow up with the students who shared in the *Sadness* bracket. This can be with a small sticky note, a short conversation without others around, or a referral to the school counselor if necessary. You do not want to do this in front of the rest of the class; you want to honor the students' privacy and feelings.
- *Timing:* Typically, this will take 45 minutes to complete.
  ○ If you have short periods, this will likely take the whole period. If you have longer blocks, take the rest of the day to do another team building game.
- *Why Play:* This game helps build empathy in the classroom as well as identifying students that need extra love and support.

Part III: A Structure to Create and Maintain Team Building—Classroom Houses

After getting to know your students' personalities, create a house system similar to the *Harry Potter* Houses.

- **Choosing house names.** It is important to select house names that are representative of your school community. When selecting house names:
  ○ Focus on all houses representing positive attributes; nothing negative!
  ○ Consider names that represent groups, people, or themes that are representative of your school community. Take time to get to know your students, their backgrounds, and their personalities before choosing house names. (If you teach multiple classes of students, you can have different names for each class.)
  ○ Ensure there is a diversity of ideas and traits represented across the houses.
  ○ Based on the class size, come up with three to five houses so you don't have more than six students per house.

- **Sorting students into houses.** After getting to know your students, you will sort your students into houses. You can use one of two approaches:
  ○ *Presort Students:* If you want to strategically place each of your students into a particular house, presort your students. When doing so, consider:
    - *Homogenous Groupings:* Do you want to group students who share similar traits? If so, ensure groupings are about personality traits and not demographic (e.g., race, ethnicity, gender, socioeconomics, etc.) traits, which could result in labeling and a segregated classroom environment.
    - *Heterogeneous Groupings:* Do you want to create groups where students represent different traits? If so, place students together who you believe will complement, support, and challenge one another.

- *Let Students Select:* Students can have a say in which house they are sorted into. If you want to give students choice, make sure you:
  - Share and discuss each house, their traits, and the meaning behind the house name and animal.
  - Let students know they can choose houses they feel a kinship to or ones they just find interesting and want to learn more about. For example, if there is a house that represents Chinese culture, (see the *Sample Houses* textbox on page 46) a Chinese student might want to select that house that honors their cultural background, *or* a student who is not culturally Chinese might want to select it because they want to learn more about Chinese culture.
  - Ask students to share a first and second choice for their houses to help with even sorting.

Sample Houses

In her class, Larissa McElrath and her coworker developed the following five houses based on cultures represented (and missing) within their school community:

Zulu—from South African culture. This house values unity, knowledge, and strength. They are very resourceful and know how to find the answers to what they are looking for. They know the importance of working together to achieve a goal. House animal: lion

Shanti—from Indian culture. Sanskrit meaning of peace. This house values calmness, focus, and positivity. They will always have a smile on their face and if something bad is going on, they are never part of the problem but are part of the solution. House animal: dove

Dharma—from Chinese culture. Important in Buddhist religion. Means truth. This house values order, respect, and righteousness. They understand the need for rules and boundaries. They will respect everyone and follow all rules. House animal: elephant

Liberty—from American culture. Means freedom. Not about being able to do whatever you want but feeling free to be yourself. This house values happiness, sensibility, and hard work. They don't cheat or look for a short cut; they work hard for what they want and don't give up. House animal: horse

Alebrije—from Spanish culture. The Alebrije are spirit guides that help you make responsible choices. This house values responsibility, reliability, and kindness. They will do the right thing because it is the right thing, not because of selfish reasons. They are someone that others can count on and rely on. House animal: dog

STRATEGY IN ACTION: CLASSROOM HOUSES—FIVE HOUSES, ONE FAMILY

In our 4th-grade classes, we create classroom houses. These are teams or base groups that students work with frequently during class and for class or grade-wide competitions.

We talk this up from Day 1. "Do you know *Harry Potter*? You are going to get sorted into houses, just like that!"

My coworker and I wait for the sorting of teams because we want to build anticipation. We also want to watch the students and see what traits each student has that will be good for each house. We want to see who will work well together.

We tell students, "When the time is right and we think you are ready to be sorted into your house, we will let you know." Kids ask up until that day. "When will you do the sorting?"

For the houses, we thought about places and cultures that were important to learn about. We thought about the demographics of our district and cultures that aren't seen. We did a lot of research to set this up to learn about words that are important in the different cultures, traits the cultures value, and what it would mean in a school setting. We talk about them being global citizens. This was such an easy way to get the kids to learn about different cultures and different people. The kids get so much from being sorted into the house.

Before the sorting ceremony, each house is explained. We share the connection to Social Studies, what the words of the house represent, the qualities of each person in that house, and the animal that symbolizes the house.

On the day of the house sorting, we use a disco light, confetti cannons, and play music to set the tone. Beforehand, I make a Google Slide that will reveal what house each student will be joining. Each student is called up when it is their turn to get sorted, the slide will play music and then reveal their house. The students all clap for each other and join their new housemates to begin connecting with each other. When we do the sorting, a lot of times, kids will note "I knew it!" when a kid gets sorted.

After each student is sorted, students will do some "icebreakers" to start team building with their housemates. They also get shirts that are their house color. The front of the shirt says, "Five Houses, One Family." From that day on, every Friday is a house spirit day. Students wear their shirts, and we also do house competitions on those days.

After sorting day, we reinforce our house motto. We end every day with a chant. EVERY DAY a student stands on the stage and leads a call and response:

Caller: Five Houses

Response: One Family

Everything else runs smoothly based on this class motto. Students need to look forward to coming to school. The fact that they know their classmates are there for them and they feel like a family is KEY!

—*Larissa McElrath*

- **Sorting Day.** Sorting day should be a celebration! Wait to host your sorting day until you feel you know your students well enough, have created and shared your house names, and considered whether you want to preselect house groups or let students decide. Then, make the day an event, as Larissa McElrath describes in *Strategy in Action: Classroom Houses—Five Houses, One Family.*

- **House games.** Once students are sorted into their groups, they need to get to know one another. This should start on Sorting Day and then extend throughout the rest of the year.
  - *Day 1:* Focus on small games that enable students to learn about one another's backgrounds, traits, connections to the house traits, etc.
  - *Weekly:* Find one day a week where you can build house competitions and team-building games into your schedule. If you have morning meetings, this can replace those on that day. The purpose of these competitions and team-building games is to build and maintain community in the classroom.

Considering Different Types of Learners

Though each of the adaptations are likely to benefit all students, the "X" marks indicate adaptations to this strategy that are particularly helpful for English-language learners, Special Education students, and Gifted and Talented students.

		English-Language Learners		
Provide visuals	Label materials in multiple languages	Translate instructions/ materials to their primary language	Model expectations/ processes	Invite students to write/speak in primary language
X		X	X	X
		Special Education Students		
Scaffold instructions/ chunking	Provide positive reinforcement	Schedule breaks	Offer multiple options/formats for student to choose	Minimize distractions
X	X			X
		Gifted and Talented Students		
Encourage students to focus on learning rather than grades	Celebrate nonacademic successes with students	Provide opportunities for students to take individualized ownership of learning	Challenge students to use more sophisticated vocabulary	Invite students to share how their thinking is extended by hearing new perspectives
X	X			

How to Implement the Strategy at Varied Grade Levels

Elementary	Middle	High
*Keep games short and simple. *Provide more structure and scaffolding for games. *Focus on games about inclusiveness and success through collaboration.	*Keep solid structure and scaffolding for the games, but give students some say in how to adapt them. *Engage in a variety of games that challenge students to explore the complexity of each of their backgrounds and find ways and spaces to become "one family."	*Make games feel age appropriate, fun, and meaningful. *Connect the games to the importance of team building that is critical to both the school setting and life outside of school.

WHY I LIKE THIS STRATEGY

I like this strategy because everyone is participating and active. In addition, it allows for learning from peers in different, game-like, formats.

—*Mindy Resnick*

I like team building games because they break the ice and it allows me to understand who the students really are personality-wise (the quiet ones, the leaders, the vocal ones, the creative ones, the rule followers/breakers, the inquisitive ones, thoughtful ones, helpful ones, disinterested ones, etc.). Doing Poker Chip Races on the first day enables me to go into day two with them where we cover the rules/expectations of the classroom, our topics of study, the structure of how we cover these topics, etc. Students understand the need for rules, expectations, structure, teamwork, individualism, and creativity in order for us to achieve success together for the semester. Poker Chip Races is a microcosm of what we will need in the classroom to have a positive and efficient day, week, month, semester.

—*Ryan McCamy*

I like using the house system as a platform for team-building games because it encourages teamwork, collaboration, and helps build relationships between the students in my class.

—*Larissa McElrath*

Adaptation for Different Assets and Needs

Class Size

Small Class
*Take time with the games to build deeper connections with one another.

*Change the makeup of groups so students get an opportunity to work with all students in the class.

Large Class
*Be efficient with your time, but take the time you need with students, even if it means sacrificing covering content for the day.

*Take good notes about what students share and what you learn about them.

Teacher Personality

Reserved/Strict
*Build in structures to the game(s) so it works for you and your comfort level.

*Simplify the game(s).

*Assign a student the job of being the game host and let them lead the show.

Outgoing/Humorous
*Embrace the role of game host and make students feel as though they are part of a really fun show they might see on TV.

*Be cognizant of ways to connect with students who are shy or introverted.

Sample Materials

1. Instructions
- Team Up
- Take note of the desk's formation
- Team Name
- Get in a row

2. Race 1 !!

3. Race 2 (1 pt)
- Chips start up front
- One at a time...front to back and then back to the front
- Person in front must raise hand when done

4. Race 3 (1pt)
- Same Rules apply
- New Rule: pass back over your left shoulder, receive over your right, face forward the whole time

5. Race 4 (1 pt)
- Same rules apply
- New Rule: no chips may hit the ground or DQ'd
- New Rule: switch seats

6. Race 5 (2pts)
- Same rules apply
- New Rule: No Talking
- New Rule: rotate arms (so now do pass back over right and receive over left)

Poker Chip Races Slides
Ryan McCarry

Race 6 (2pts)

- Same rules apply.
- New Rule: one different color chip added, that chip must be passed with the opposite arms (pass back over left, receive over right)

Race 7/8 (3pts)

- Same rules apply.
- New Rule: remove different color chip
- New Rule: Eyes Closed

Race 9 (2pts, tiebreaker)

- Same rules apply
- New Rule: eyes open, pick a shoulder, switch order?
- New Rule: Pure Speed!!!!

Do Now:

- Compare and contrast the beginning of the activity to the end of the activity?
- Provide adjectives to describe the first race.
- What change took place that allowed for the Race 1 and Race 7 to be so different?
- What did you need to do to be successful?
- What was the overall objective of yesterday's race activity?

Debrief/Classroom connections

- Chips drop (not always perfect)
- Presented with a difficult task but had to overcome it (extra chip)
- Honesty/Integrity eyes closed
- Efficiency: don't need to sprint all the time, but we need to get started on time and be efficient with our time together...

- Get 1% better everyday.
- Sharpen our edge each day.
- Don't you think you did better without talking?
- When given the opportunity for pure speed, who stepped up? Who was creative? Who led?

- Do these same traits relate to other areas of life?

Poker Chip Races Slides
Ryan McCarry

Chapter 3

Routines

In this chapter you will find strategies for creating and sustaining routines that support positive classroom climate. These include:

- Creating **Classroom Jobs** (Strategy 9) to help students come together as a community, teach responsibility, and takes some of the pressure off teachers.

    Assigning classroom jobs allows me to focus more on the actual teaching, instead of some of the more mundane tasks (erasing the board, passing papers out, collecting papers, etc.). Students become more invested in the classroom experience, and therefore learning.

    —*Robert Boyce*, chapter contributor

- Using **Check-Ins** (Strategy 10) to meet students where they are in their lives before engaging in academic requirements.

    Checking in with students promotes the understanding that our classroom is comprised of all students and teachers working together. Everyone's voice is important.

    —*Jordan Griffiths*, chapter contributor

- Inviting **Student Voice to Start Class** (Strategy 11) and celebrating, honoring, and respecting students' lived experiences and perspectives.

    Kids like structure and knowing what they're walking into each day. It's a predictable routine and safe structure and they appreciate that each day starts with valuing their thoughts and feelings.

    —*Marta O'Brien*, chapter contributor

- **Working the Room** (Strategy 12) by using the physical space in the classroom to ensure that students are engaged throughout the lesson.

  > With a focus on the physical classroom and connecting with each student, routines, classroom arrangement, movement during class, and chances for conversations are all important tools that can easily be incorporated into daily instruction.
  >
  > —*Mary Eldredge-Sandbo*, chapter contributor

- Integrating **Brain and Body Breaks** (Strategy 13) into each day so students and you can reengage and focus during a school day that is often physically, emotionally, and psychologically draining.

  > Brain and body breaks are great because they help you step away from the curriculum and help students increase their focus and energy.
  >
  > —*Pamela Goff*, chapter contributor

- **Mindfulness** practices (Strategy 14) to build self-awareness and self-management.

  > Mindfulness practice is an investment in education. More importantly, it's an investment in these kids understanding themselves.
  >
  > —*TJ Belasco*, chapter contributor

- **Spotlighting Students** (Strategy 15) to celebrate peers' successes and gain a clear sense of expectations and positive next steps.

  > Something about students seeing their work on the screen in front of the whole class makes the work somehow more meaningful.
  >
  > —*Janice Wilke*, chapter contributor

HIGHLIGHTS

- In **Classroom Jobs** (Strategy 9), check out Sarah Cullom's Job Wheel, which helps ensure students get equal chances to have different jobs throughout the year.
- See how to focus on students' feelings and their readiness for learning in **Check-Ins** (Strategy 10).
- Learn about *Minute Gifts*, a way for students to share their ideas, interests, talents, and experiences with the class in **Student Voice to Start Class** (Strategy 11).
- Find prompts that make the checking in with students meaningful during group or individual work in **Working the Room** (Strategy 12).
- Choose from lists of brain and body breaks that are grounding or energizing in **Brain and Body Breaks** (Strategy 13).
- Learn about mindful breathing practices used by teachers, students, and athletes in **Mindfulness** (Strategy 14).
- Find out ways to create a culture of sharing in **Spotlighting Students** (Strategy 15).

GUIDING QUESTIONS

As you read through this chapter, consider the following:

1. In what ways do students see themselves as productive contributors to our class environment?
2. How can I check in with my students personally and academically? How do I follow up on what I learn about students?
3. How can I elevate and celebrate students' voices in the classroom?
4. What do I want to learn and share with students when I work the room, and how can I do so effectively?
5. In what ways can I assess and meet my students' needs for grounding or energizing?
6. What are my intentions for using mindfulness with my students? How are my choices helping set us on a course for meeting those intentions?
7. What are the best ways to celebrate and spotlight my students' successes?

STRATEGY 9: CLASSROOM JOBS

> Teacher Contributors
> *Robert Boyce, West Windsor-Plainsboro High School North (NJ), 9th–12th grades*
> *Sarah Cullom, Dublin Elementary School (CA), 4th grade*

Classroom jobs help students come together as a community, teach responsibility, and take some of the pressure off teachers. Jobs can range in demand and importance. Think of all of the things you do in a given day. What could students help with? When students take on classroom jobs, your job gets easier and they feel a sense of pride and belonging.

Strategy Implementation

1. **Create jobs.** Once you determine how many jobs you want to have in your classroom, there are several ways to create classroom jobs.
   - *Determine How Many Jobs You Want to Create:* Ask yourself:
     - Do I want each student to have a job at all times?
     - Do I want to select students to rotate through a smaller set of jobs?
     - What will I do if I have more jobs than students?
   - *Develop a List of Jobs:* To do this:
     - Reflect on your day. Determine what particular jobs you can outsource to students.
     - Ask colleagues about jobs they have in their classrooms. (See Sarah Cullom's Job Wheel in *Sample Materials* on page 61.)
     - Invite students to develop a job list.

   > No matter if it's big or small, every job a student does saves me time, while making students feel special and included.
   > —*Sarah Cullom*

2. **Determine how jobs get assigned.** You might use different job assignment methods as the year progresses. Random selection or contests are fun for the start of the year when you don't know students well. As the year progresses, you may want to assign jobs based on students' related strengths or areas for growth. Job selections methods include:
   - *Random Selection:* Pull names out of a hat, assign jobs by number, or by distributing index cards with the jobs listed on the.
   - *Game Show Style:* Determine the order of who gets to choose their jobs based on who wins a low-pressure contest or answers a riddle correctly.
   - *Teacher Assigned:* You choose who will do the jobs based on how the jobs will enhance students' confidence or help them develop skills.
   - *Job Rotation:* Jobs are assigned via a rotation schedule, so every student gets a chance to do each job once before the jobs are assigned in a second round. This works well when you have an equal number of jobs and students.

   > Erasing the board takes physical effort. One year, I held a cartwheel competition for the job of board eraser.
   > —*Robert Boyce*

> **Unusual Classroom Jobs**
>
> A description of some of the more unusual jobs that I have in my classroom follows.
>
> **Attendance Monitor:** Puts an *Absent Folder* on students' desks who are absent. Any papers passed out that day go in their folder for when they return.
> **Homework Monitor:** Writes down the homework on a sticky note for a student who is absent and leaves it on their desk for when they return.
> **Safety Monitor:** Passes out wipes to clean desks, hand sanitizer to keep hands clean, and carries the emergency backpack out during fire drills (and holds the all clear sign up on the playground for the principal to see).
> **Class Photographer:** When I started this job, I gave the class photographer a disposable camera. They took it home and took 8–9 pictures of their family, community, activities they like to do or anything that was special to them. After three weeks and three students taking pictures, I would develop the pictures and put them up on a special bulletin board. I've changed it a little now so students take pictures at school of important activities, spirit days, etc. using my phone.
> **Bruin Babysitter:** Since I went to UCLA, I have a stuffed Bruin Bear. When I started teaching, he would go home in a rolling backpack with a journal and students would get to "babysit" him for the week. They would write in the journal about what he did with them and return the backpack with the bear and journal the following Monday. There was one rule that Bruin Bear had to sleep in his backpack and couldn't sleep in bed with the student. I've changed this job since then and now, instead of going home, he sits on their desk for the week, as our class mascot.
> **Student of the Week:** Can bring in something special to share with the class and fills out a survey that's read to the class about their likes. The class makes a book for them (each student fills out a page) with compliments about the student of the week and a picture.
>
> —*Sarah Cullom*

- *Volunteers:* Students can simply volunteer for jobs. You may do a first-come first-serve or pick a name out of a jar of names of volunteers. This works well when assigning extra jobs if you have more jobs than students. If you have more volunteers than extra jobs, you might say that students can't have a job two weeks in a row.

3. **Job training.** Teach the full class about what each job involves. Methods of training include:
   - *Jobs Poster:* List all jobs with brief descriptions and images.
   - *Job ID Cards:* Create an ID card for each job with the job description. This can be kept in students' folders or on lanyards like the teacher wears.
   - *Job BINGO:* Create BINGO cards with each job title. Read out descriptions of each job. This is a fun way to learn about jobs and work on listening skills.

- *On-the-Spot:* Students can learn and improve their job performance on the spot by adapting what they are doing. Stop them when you want to change their approach. Praise choices that increase efficiency. This is a great chance for students to explore how they can support each other in their roles (e.g., The attendance taker can pass absent students' folders to the paper distributor who can place copies of the day's handouts in each absentee's folder.).
- *Peer-to-Peer:* After the initial group of students has performed their jobs for the first time, you can ask them to train the next students who will have those jobs.

4. **Maintaining quality control.** When students take on classroom jobs, this is a chance for them to show responsibility and develop skills. It's also a way to take some of the work off your hands. That said, if jobs aren't done well, the results won't be positive. To maintain quality control, incorporate:
   - *Student Self-Checks:* Ask students to rate themselves. Think Uber or restaurant ratings. Would they give themselves four out of four stars? If not, what do they need to improve?
   - *Class Feedback:* Taking on a job is a way to contribute to the classroom community. Give students a chance to provide feedback. (See how Robert Boyce did this with a class supreme court in *Strategy in Action: An Efficient Learning Community* on page 58.)
   - *Teacher Feedback:* Take the time to let students know how their efforts are impacting you. Are you more productive because of the time you are saving thanks to their great work? Do you need them to put in a bit more effort? Clear and pointed feedback leads to best results.

What if a Student Doesn't Want to Take on a Job?

- Ask the student why they don't want to do the job.
- Help the student get more comfortable doing the job by modeling how to do it or have a peer who has previously done the job serve as a mentor.
- Remind the student that the job is temporary.
- If the student really doesn't want to do the job, get a new volunteer to cover that job.
- Consider developing a trade system. This student will take your job if you take theirs.

Jobs are expected because we're working together as a team. Everyone has to pitch in for our class to run smoothly.

—Sarah Cullom

STRATEGY IN ACTION: AN EFFICIENT LEARNING COMMUNITY

During my first years of teaching, I found I was burdened down with erasing the board, handing out papers, and putting homework in the folders. I had enough to do with teaching math. I needed to find a way to get my students invested in helping, so I developed a list of classroom jobs.

I told students that if they could maintain a job the entire marking period, they would get extra credit points proportional to their job performance as monitored by me and the class president. We rated students' job performance on a scale of 0–10. No student ever received a 0 or 1 because if they were doing that poorly, they were fired. In any given marking period students worked toward approximately 600 total points for their overall grade based on homework, classwork, tests, quizzes, and projects; therefore, the 10 points of extra credit had little if any impact on their grade, but the experience of taking on a classroom job increased their engagement in the class and ability to take on responsibility.

Sometimes students would resign, and I would have to hire a new person for the job. Sometimes students would do a job so well that they would want to do it again. The class had a say in the development of the various jobs. After a few years of doing this, I appointed students to be judges on a classroom supreme court because students wanted to appeal to modify the job of paper passer to only involve papers that weren't graded.

The supreme court became an important part of this system alongside the president. The president would rate the job performance of each class employee. These reports were often pretty funny to read with comical descriptions of successes and failures. The supreme court was available to any student who wanted to appeal a decision in relation to job performance or job description.

The most important and challenging job was the temp. This person had to know all of the jobs in the classroom and jump in whenever students who had these jobs were absent. I had a student who was by far the finest temp I ever saw. She would come to class and already know who was absent. One day, she had to do four jobs. She was so good, the supreme court let her have the job all year.

A favorite job was the assessment assistant. Two or three students would take on this role and team with me to develop assessments for the class. These students also were in charge of reminding students about upcoming assessments and giving an overview of what to expect. Hands down, this was the most sought-after job in my classroom.

At the start of the school year, students would enter my class asking about jobs. Many said that my class was the most organized classroom they'd ever been in. That's because we kept it running efficiently. If students weren't doing their jobs, they were fired. The president and supreme court took on quality control. I created this system as a way to give me optimal time for focusing on math. The benefits I saw were far greater. Students learned responsibility. The class became its own functioning community, and we had fun in the process.

—*Robert Boyce*

Considering Different Types of Learners

Though each of the adaptations are likely to benefit all students, the "X" marks indicate adaptations to this strategy that are particularly helpful for English-language learners, Special Education students, and Gifted and Talented students.

English-Language Learners				
Provide visuals	Label materials in multiple languages	Translate instructions/ materials to their primary language	Model expectations/ processes	Invite students to write/speak in primary language
X	X	X	X	

Special Education Students				
Scaffold instructions/ chunking	Provide positive reinforcement	Schedule breaks	Offer multiple options/formats for student to choose	Minimize distractions
X	X			X

Gifted and Talented Students				
Encourage students to focus on learning rather than grades	Celebrate nonacademic successes with students	Provide opportunities for students to take individualized ownership of learning	Challenge students to use more sophisticated vocabulary	Invite students to share how their thinking is extended by hearing new perspectives
X	X			

WHY I LIKE THIS STRATEGY

Assigning classroom jobs allows me to focus more on the actual teaching, instead of some of the more mundane tasks (erasing the board, passing papers out, collecting papers, etc.). Students become more invested in the classroom experience and therefore learning. And they enjoy the whole thing, especially when there are grievances filed with our Supreme Court.

—*Robert Boyce*

I feel that giving a job to every student in the class creates a class community where every child is important to our classroom and to our day-to-day business.

—*Sarah Cullom*

How to Implement the Strategy at Varied Grade Levels

Elementary	Middle	High
*Read books about jobs in the community like *The Barrio* to emphasize the importance of everyone contributing. *Incorporate *Student of the Week* into your jobs list or rotation, so students can see when their turn is coming up.	*Create a small list of jobs and rotate groups of students through them. Because classes aren't a full day, it makes more sense to do this. *Be sure to include jobs that highlight students' strengths.	*Give students an opportunity to reflect on how the class operates and design a list of jobs. *Discuss how noting what needs doing and taking action are skills that are correlated with job and financial success after high school.

Adaptation for Different Assets and Needs

Class Size

Small Class
*Select jobs based on the number of students you have in class (or the maximum number you have if teaching multiple periods.)
*Offer more than one job to each student.

Large Class
*Determine which jobs might be better completed in partners or teams. (e.g., The Materials Distributor could be expanded to four to five students, one per table.)
*Determine with the class the jobs that will help things run efficiently for your class.

Time

Limited Time
*Remember that assigning classroom jobs may actually give you back time. Once students know how to do their jobs and do them well, you may find yourself with more time on your hands!
*Practice doing the jobs quickly and efficiently to be sure that they are helping you all save time.

Lots of Time
*Take time for job training and to reflect on how well the classroom community is functioning regarding classroom jobs.
*Reflect on how each job enhances skills that students can use outside of class. Jobs not only enhance and improve community, but they can also support students' transfer of skills.

STRATEGY IN ACTION: A JOB WHEEL

I use a Job Wheel to assign classroom jobs to my students. The wheel has 32 jobs, so each student gets a new job every week and it rotates one spot every Monday. Students can see what jobs they'll have next and how many weeks until a special job like *Student of the Week*.

I created the Job Wheel (with the help of Kinko's) during my first or second year teaching. I was teaching at a Title I school in Los Angeles where there was a high transiency rate. I created the job "Welcome Team" because I was constantly getting new students who needed help around the school or classroom and someone to play with at recess. I remember being new to a school in 4th grade and the teacher asked a student to show me around at recess. She was my best friend for the next five years.

Another favorite job I use is *Classroom Host*. That student quietly gets up from their desk when a guest (like the principal) comes into our class. The *Classroom Host* greets the visitor at the door by introducing themself with their name, shakes their hand, and tells the guest what the class is working on or learning about. Sometimes the guest has questions or wants to see their work. When they're done, the student sits down and rejoins the lesson. Principals love this job!

Whether students have jobs like those described or they are the classroom sweeper that week, they know they are helping their classroom community, and are usually excited to do so.

—Sarah Cullom

Sample Materials

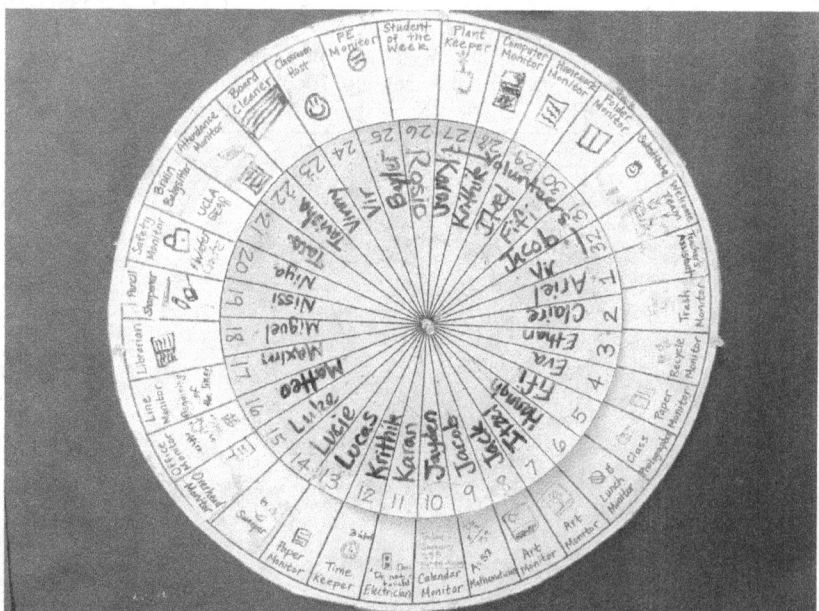

Job Wheel
Sarah Cullom

STRATEGY 10: CHECK-INS

> **Teacher Contributors**
> *Andrew Curtin, Bishop Ireton High School (VA), 11th–12th grades*
> *Jordan Griffiths, The American School of Kuwait (Kuwait), 3rd grade*

Check-ins are a way to get to know students individually and to meet them where they are in their lives before engaging in academic requirements. Posing questions and developing connections with students as individuals helps them feel seen and validated.

Strategy Implementation

1. **Be intentional.** Consistently keep the importance of developing relationships with students in mind when allocating time, developing plans, and making decisions on the spot. Make clear why you prioritize checking in.

   > I'm intentional about building strong relationships with students through check-ins. They often come to me with their worries, concerns, excitement, etc.
   >
   > —*Jordan Griffith*

2. **Model how to check in.** Be transparent about your emotions as the teacher and how you are managing them or about how ready you are to try something new. Public, in-the-moment, check-ins are excellent opportunities for modeling.

3. **Start before the bell.** Check in with students as they enter your classroom. Much can be quickly ascertained by making eye contact and saying hello. Read body language. Ask about their day. Comment on a pair of sneakers or fidget toy they are carrying. All of this opens up space for making a connection with your students.

   > There's so much emphasis on bell-to-bell, but if you engage with students *before* the bell, that's where I find I have the most success.
   >
   > —*Andrew Curtin*

4. **Make check-ins part of class routine.** Check-ins are helpful at many points during the class. Find times within your class routine that make sense for consistently integrating check-ins:
   - Start of class
   - During transitions
   - After learning something new
   - End of class

5. **Make time and opportunity for private check-ins.** Some students may not be comfortable sharing how they are doing with the whole class. When students are working independently, take time to individually check in with those who might

---

Sample Check-Ins

Feelings
- Share one word to describe your day.
- Share a color that connects with your feelings.
- Tell how one of the things you are currently wearing reflects how you are feeling today.
- Share something you've been thinking about or talking about a lot lately.
- Draw the weather forecast that represents how you feel.
- Look at several visuals (could be emojis, animals with different expressions, etc.) and choose how one connects with your feelings.

Readiness
- Ratings Scales: On a scale of 1–4 (1 = low, 4 = high) respond:
  - What's your energy level?
  - What's your focus level?
  - What's your confidence level for today's work?
- Questions
  - How well are you able to focus today?
  - What's distracting you today?
  - What's helping you focus?

---

not have shared. (For more on how to do this individually and in small groups, see *Strategy 12: Working the Room*.) You can create opportunities throughout your lesson for students to share through writing or drawing. These may include:

- *What I Want You to Know:* Students complete a handout that includes space for writing or drawing what they want teachers to know and a checkbox at the bottom indicating whether they want their teacher to facilitate further conversation with other teachers, counselors, or parents.
  - *Personal Check-In Page:* Students complete responses to check-in questions on a page or electronic form. They can opt to share out loud or hand it in directly to you. (See sample *Check-In Form* in *Sample Materials* on page 67.)
  - *Non-Check-In Check-In:* Sometimes a student doesn't want to be asked if they are OK. They may not be ready to talk about how they are feeling or what is going on, but that doesn't mean that they don't want to connect. You can do a *non-check-in check-in* by simply asking them about something you know they are interested in or sharing that you were thinking about them when [fill in the blank]. This opens up a door for communication when the student is ready.

6. **Keep making time.** Once you begin to make these connections with students, they may start checking in outside of class time. Think about ways to structure your day to allow for flexibility, so you can be present with students when they need you.

Considering Different Types of Learners

Though each of the adaptations are likely to benefit all students, the "X" marks indicate adaptations to this strategy that are particularly helpful for English-language learners, Special Education students, and Gifted and Talented students.

		English-Language Learners		
Provide visuals	Label materials in multiple languages	Translate instructions/ materials to their primary language	Model expectations/ processes	Invite students to write/speak in primary language
X		X	X	
		Special Education Students		
Scaffold instructions/ chunking	Provide positive reinforcement	Schedule breaks	Offer multiple options/formats for student to choose	Minimize distractions
X	X		X	
		Gifted and Talented Students		
Encourage students to focus on learning rather than grades	Celebrate nonacademic successes with students	Provide opportunities for students to take individualized ownership of learning	Challenge students to use more sophisticated vocabulary	Invite students to share how their thinking is extended by hearing new perspectives
X	X			X

STRATEGY IN ACTION: THE STORY BEHIND THE GRADE

I was confused about this one student who was a really talented writer and whose homework was always done to a very high level of completion, but she bombed the first test of the year. I happened to bump into her in the hallway after school and decided to ask, "Hey, can we talk about this test for a second?" Tears welled up immediately, and she shared that she had really terrible test anxiety. She would study for hours, but on test day, her understanding just disappeared. Knowing that, we came up with a plan to try to manage the anxiety, build confidence, and prepare for future tests.

Honestly, though while we reviewed specific strategies for studying and writing, I don't think the techniques were really what turned it around. Rather it was just that I took the time to find out what was going on and reached out to support her—it boosted her confidence to know someone cared and believed in her. If I hadn't checked in with her informally in the hallway, I would never have known what she needed or how to connect with the student to help her be successful.

—*Andrew Curtin*

How to Implement the Strategy at Varied Grade Levels

Elementary	Middle	High
*Create a Coping Corner, a space where students can go to gather their thoughts and reflect on their emotions. This may include a page on which they can draw or write how they are feeling and share with their teacher, counselor, or caretaker.	*Because this is a time when students are working with multiple teachers for different subjects, you may want to ask them about their favorite ways of checking in during other classes and adapt those other check-ins to fit your class.	*Ask students to lead check-ins. If this is part of your classroom or school culture, they will likely have some favorite approaches and may be eager to diversify this experience.
*Share feelings charts with faces and descriptors to help students develop a shared language during check-ins.	*Meet with students in small groups rather than as a full-class for check-ins. They may be more open to sharing.	*Connect check-ins with the importance of maintaining positive mental health habits. Encourage students to think about ways they can check in with themselves regarding self-care, healthy choices, and next steps.

WHY I LIKE THIS STRATEGY

I believe a strong classroom community forms the basis for all learning, growth, and development that occurs. I think that community building cannot be rushed, and must be valued. Checking in with students promotes the understanding that our classroom is comprised of all students and teachers working together. Everyone's voice is important.

—*Jordan Griffiths*

Not only do I believe that this strategy is better for students, but it makes teaching a lot more fun for me as the teacher as well! I really enjoy each of my different classes, and this approach helps keep each period of the day fresh—yes, it might be the fourth time I'm teaching a lesson on the radical phase of Reconstruction, but when I've gotten to know my students well and can shape the lesson to what speaks specifically to them, each period is a little different and they're all more interesting. Students respond really well to the feeling that teachers are taking the time to tailor lessons and classroom conversations to their interests, even a little bit.

—*Andrew Curtin*

Adaptation for Different Assets and Needs

Student Personality	
Reserved	**Open**
*Create opportunities for private sharing through writing or drawing.	*Sometimes students want to share, and share, and share! When this overtakes time set for academic learning, suggest a journal or a writing/drawing page that students can use and share with you at a later time.
*Model sharing for students. When they see you share, they may be more willing to share.	
*Use stories to spark conversation and connection.	*Ask these students to encourage their quieter classmates to share during check-ins.

Time	
Limited Time	**Lots of Time**
*Remember that giving two to three minutes at the start of class for checking in will improve the quality of the remaining time. Students will be more focused and engaged when they feel that they are cared for and they are part of a classroom community.	*Add more community building activities (see *Strategy 8: Team-Building Games* and *Strategy 17: Building Peer-to-Peer Relationships and Trust*) so students feel comfortable and trust one another when they engage in check-ins.
*Make an effort to connect with and check in with students before and after class as well as when you see them around the school or outside of school.	*Explicitly build check-ins into your routine at multiple points during your lesson (beginning, middle, or end).

STRATEGY IN ACTION: THE POWER OF COMMUNITY

I started really focusing on using check-ins to help build my classroom community when I began at my current school (this will be my fourth year). Having grown up in an International School environment, I understand how important it is that all students feel welcome, supported, and heard in the classroom.

I believe that when students feel that their peers and teachers care and support them, then negative behaviors decrease. I really noticed this in my first year at my current school. Of the six classes in my grade level, two of us really prioritized building relationships. In those classrooms, there were less behavioral referrals, higher academic achievement, and students generally collaborated well together.

I noticed that my students would often look out for each other at recess, and want to help each other in any way they could. For example, in my first year I had a student who broke both of his legs. My students would always look out for him, they would come over to him at recess and check in on him, they'd be quick to move their desks, etc., so he could move freely through the classroom. I was so impressed how they thought of each other, and his mother came to me crying, thanking me for allowing him to feel accepted. Initially, he hadn't wanted to come to school for fear of being excluded.

I truly believe in the power of this community. I have had numerous parents throughout my year tell me their child has never been so happy at school. Students who were bullied in previous years were given a chance to flourish, and it makes me incredibly happy.

—*Jordan Griffiths*

Sample Materials

Weekly Check In

Please respond to the prompts below by 8am on Friday.
(1-2 sentences or bullet points per prompt is fine. Also, happy to read more!)

Name
Short answer text

What's going well?
Long answer text

What concerns do you have?
Long answer text

OPTIONAL: Anything else you think I should know in order to best support you. (This can be about your fieldwork or your experiences outside of school)
Long answer text

Check-In Form
Maureen Connolly

STRATEGY 11: STUDENT VOICE TO START CLASS

> Teacher Contributors
> Marta O'Brien, Guardian Angels Catholic School (FL), 6th–8th grades
> Annie Thoms, Stuyvesant High School (NY), 9th–12th grades

Starting class with student voice lets students know that the class is theirs, makes them the center of the learning from the outset, and provides ways to celebrate, honor, and respect students' lived experiences and perspectives. Student voice can be related to the class content or connected to students' lives, or a combination of the two.

Strategy Implementation

There are multiple ways a teacher can start class with students' voices. The strategies presented are tied to personal sharing, reviewing prior learning, or grappling with the content or theme of the day. Any or all of these strategies can be used consistently in your classroom.

> **Student Voice Helps Build Community and Trust!**
>
> My classes range in size from 28 to 34 students and it's common for students not to know each other as human beings. In some non-English Language Arts classes they don't even get to know each other's names. Starting class with students' voices is a real opportunity to have a classroom where students are comfortable writing about personal things, sharing personal content, having rich text-based discussions, and it allows for students to get to know each other as people.
>
> —Annie Thoms

Part I: Personal Share—Quick Write and Author's Chair to Start Class

There are many ways to start class by having students share their thoughts and ideas. Morning meetings have become a common approach. Methods to keep students engaged and vocal during morning meetings or any other routine that has been established to encourage student voice to start class are quick writes and giving students an Author's Chair. This entails:

1. **Make it a routine.** Starting class each day in the same way with doing a quick write that highlights students' voices is important to help students know that their thinking and experiences will be valued each day. This makes it easier to get them onboard for what they are doing the rest of

> Kids like structure and knowing what they're walking into each day. It's a predictable routine and safe structure and they appreciate that each day starts with valuing their thoughts and feelings.
>
> —Marta O'Brien

class. They start class with a space that is for them and then they are open to the teacher engaging them in academic content.

2. **Daily theme.** Create a daily theme for the quick writes where students know what to expect each day. These themes could be related to your content areas (e.g., as an English Language Arts teacher you might do *Metaphor Monday*), emotional well-being (e.g., *Motivational Monday*), or any other themes that you believe will excite your students. Consider developing themes *with* your students as part of your routines and culture building at the beginning of the year, and then as the year progresses, let students suggest ways to switch up the themes.
   - NOTE: You can personalize the theme for each class you teach if you have different classes.

3. **Go over the prompt.** Take time to go over your daily quick write prompt with the entire class before they begin. Ensure all students are clear on the expectations and timing for the quick write before they start.

> **Switch Up Quick Writes!**
>
> You can keep the routine of doing quick writes without having students write the same way every day. Consider having students:
>
> - Draw their thoughts.
> - Perform or verbally share thoughts.
> - Write in various forms like poetry, song lyrics, bullet points, etc.

4. **Be part of the process.** While students work, be an active participant in one of three ways:
   - *Write with the Students:* It is often great for students to see that you are "in it" with them and doing what they are doing. This will enable you to share your voice after hearing from students.
   - *Conference with the Students:* Take the opportunity to have one-on-one check-ins with students who need support.
   - *Work the Room:* Even if you decide to write yourself or conference with students, make time to circulate the room to check on and support students in the class.

5. **Author's Chair.** Give students the Author's Chair (which can be an actual chair designated somewhere in the room) to share their thoughts and initiate class dialogue. The sharing process includes:
   - *Modeling:* Early in the year, consider modeling how to share with the class after you complete the quick write, and how to engage the class in dialogue around what was shared.
   - *Sharing:* Have a handful of students (depending on time) volunteer to share.
     - *Author:* Students either read directly from or paraphrase what they wrote.
     - *Listening Students:* All eyes are on the author. Take notes on what they

> Because the focus is on students first and they are being listened to, they are more willing to buy-in. Students really appreciate that.
>
> —Marta O'Brien

love, questions they have, and what they think could be adapted or changed (if the writing exercise is about craft and not just ideas). Find ways to show empathy and support for what they are sharing, and reinforce what is valuable and important about what was shared.
- NOTE: If many students want to share, have them share in small groups and then groups can nominate a few students to share with the entire class.
- *Appreciation:* As a class, come up with some form of *positive affirmation* to celebrate what the author shared (claps, snaps, jazz hands, etc.).
- *Dialogue:* After each author shares, have students, based on their notes, raise questions or share something they connected with to engage the author and the rest of the class in a quick discussion. If you are trying to keep the sharing short, only have a couple of students engage in the dialogue before going to the next author; however, if a topic or theme arises that needs the time, take it!

> Once you know someone's story, the dynamic of the class changes.
> —Marta O'Brien

6. **Transition to your day's lesson.** If you are going directly from your Author's Chair to the heart of your lesson, find a way to connect what you discussed during the quick write sharing with what you will be focusing on for the day. This might be a content connection or a skills or dispositions connection.

STRATEGY IN ACTION: QUICK WRITES TO INITIATE STUDENT VOICE

One of the concepts I teach my students is that the idea for a story or poem could be found anywhere, be it a writing prompt, a roll of the Metaphor Dice (created by Taylor Mali), or a mentor text. Quick writes are one tool that can help you build a writing piece. When paired with other tools in their writer's toolbox such as word choice, sensory details, and figurative language, quick writes can send you on your way. Quick writes allow students to write at their own level and at their own pace. This strategy strengthens students' writing and speaking skills. It exposes them to writing from their peers and creates a community where they can give and receive feedback. It fosters an environment where students can share and build rapport with classmates. When students discover a genre or style of writing or when they are excited to share in the Author's Chair, it serves as confirmation to me that this strategy works.

—Marta O'Brien

Part II: Review Prior Learning—Minutes and Minutes Gift to Start Class

Many teachers like to start class by reviewing material from previous lessons, but it doesn't need to be teacher-centered; rather, make it a space to honor and hear students' voices! One strategy to do this is using Minutes and Minutes Gifts.

1. **Explain minutes to students.** Let students know that minutes are often taken at meetings in professional settings to remind people of their progress and what has been discussed previously. Explain that the format for class minutes will be a paragraph summarizing the previous day's aim and key takeaways that a student reads aloud to start class. The summary should identify the most important moment of class, which for example, might include a direct quote from a student during a class discussion.

   > Periods are 42 minutes at my school and students shift gears a ton; therefore, Minutes provides a moment of transition and easing into the class. It also highlights and emphasizes the importance of classroom community: discussion is about the students talking with each other, not just about the teacher talking to them.
   >
   > —Annie Thoms

2. **Every student participates.** Provide students with a minutes sign-up sheet at the start of each month or marking period. Students are required to sign up at least twice.

3. **Make the sign-up sheet visible and accessible.** Post the sign-up in an easily accessible place in the classroom like a wall that is not obstructed by tables or desks. If you use a digital platform like Google Classroom, post the sign-up sheet there as well.

4. **Preparing the minutes.** Students will be reminded the day before they are in charge of presenting. They are responsible for writing out their summary paragraph before coming to class the next day. The assigned minutes-taker may:
   - Jot down notes about main takeaways from class during the closing activity the day before they present.
   - Complete the paragraph before going to bed so the day's content is fresh in their mind.
   - Share their paragraph with you for feedback before they present; but let students know they must submit the paragraph the evening before presenting if they want feedback.

5. **Share the minutes and minutes gift.** At the start of class, the minutes presenter shares their minutes and minutes gift. In total, the minutes and minutes gift should take three to five minutes and include:
   - *Get Ready:* Standing up either at their seat or in front of the class based on their comfort level.
     - NOTE: If a minutes presenter forgets their minutes, ask for *impromptu Minutes* from a volunteer student and then ask the student who was supposed to do the minutes to perform a brief interpretive dance of your choosing (jellyfish or pigeon hunting for crumbs are good ones), so long as the student is

> **STRATEGY IN ACTION: STARTING CLASS WITH MINUTE GIFTS**
>
> I have used minutes in my classroom for more than 20 years, at all high school grade levels.
>
> In one 9th-grade class, a boy who struggled for much of the semester to keep his temper and to respond to peers with positive feedback folded and distributed an origami crane to each member of the class as a keepsake. In one 11th-grade class, a girl wrote a song about her classmates and sang and played it on her ukulele. In one 12th-grade class, a boy explained why he had become vegan and made us all zucchini *noodles* with tomato sauce. Later, I learned he had convinced two other students in the class to become vegan as well. In one 9th-grade class, a girl choreographed and performed a dance representing her understanding of the protagonist's relationship to water in Jamaica Kincaid's novel *Annie John*, which we had just finished reading.
>
> In each of these cases, the minutes gift allowed students to share something meaningful and get to know each other in a deeper way. When we reflect on the class at the end of each semester, minutes gifts are often some of the joyful memories.
>
> —*Annie Thoms*

      amenable; then the student who forgot should be signed up for a new day to present, possibly replacing the student who volunteered in their stead.
- *Reminder for Next Class:* Remind the next day's minutes presenter that it will be their turn to share the minutes the following class.
- *Minutes:* Read the minutes summary. This should take no more than two to three minutes to read.
- *Minutes Gift:* This is a demonstration of a passion (karate, dance, playing the trumpet), a book recommendation, food they've made from scratch, or facts about the author of a book you're reading, etc. The demonstration should take no more than two minutes.
- *Appreciation:* As a class, come up with some form of *positive affirmation* to celebrate what the minutes presenter shared (claps, snaps, jazz hands, etc.).

6. **Debriefing the minutes or minutes gift.** Depending on timing and how enticing the minutes gift is to the class, leave a minute to debrief the minutes or gift and give the rest of the class space to react to what was presented. This will encourage additional student voices to launch the class into the day's lesson.

7. **Transition to your day's lesson.** If you are going directly from your minutes presentations to the heart of your lesson, find a way to connect what you discussed during the minutes, thus bridging the content from the day before with the learning of today.

Part III: Connecting with the Content or Theme for the Day

Another great way to celebrate students' voices to start class is to do opening activities that are meaningful and relevant to students' lives and make a direct connection to the theme for the day. To do this:

1. **Find a connection.** Look closely at your curriculum for the day and find something about the content or theme that will be meaningful to your students and relevant to their lives.

2. **Design the opening activity.** Design an activity that engages *all* students with the connection you discovered.

3. **Give multiple students time to share.** It is important to give space and time for multiple students (ideally different students each day) to share their connection to the activity. Be the facilitator and encourage students to respond to and build on one another's ideas. This helps elevate students' voices, perspectives, and experiences.

4. **Transition.** Connect the students' shared experiences and perspectives to the content/theme for the day as you move into the heart of your lesson.

Considering Different Types of Learners

Though each of the adaptations are likely to benefit all students, the "X" marks indicate adaptations to this strategy that are particularly helpful for English-language learners, Special Education students, and Gifted and Talented students.

WHY I LIKE THIS STRATEGY

This activity allows for a variety of topics, genres, and styles to be introduced to students. It "forces" them to focus on a single idea for several minutes and write freely. It engages students immediately as they enter the classroom, serves as a spark for their creativity, builds writing stamina, organically establishes the need for revision, and fosters community among the students.

—*Marta O'Brien*

Class starts with a student voice, not my voice. Students get to know each other better, and I get to know them. I get a sense of what students actually took away from each day's class. We collect the minutes in a folder so absent students can use them to review. I can (and have, at some points) grade and respond to some minutes pages to ensure that they're all really effective summaries—make it more of a writing assignment or assessment.

—*Annie Thoms*

English-Language Learners				
Provide visuals	Label materials in multiple languages	Translate instructions/ materials to their primary language	Model expectations/ processes	Invite students to write/speak in primary language
		X	X	
Special Education Students				
Scaffold instructions/ chunking	Provide positive reinforcement	Schedule breaks	Offer multiple options/formats for student to choose	Minimize distractions
X	X		X	X
Gifted and Talented Students				
Encourage students to focus on learning rather than grades	Celebrate nonacademic successes with students	Provide opportunities for students to take individualized ownership of learning	Challenge students to use more sophisticated vocabulary	Invite students to share how their thinking is extended by hearing new perspectives
X	X	X		

How to Implement the Strategy at Varied Grade Levels

Elementary	Middle	High
*Have students represent their ideas and thoughts through images, verbal sharing, and performances rather than writing. *Make topics for opening activities age-appropriate with fewer choices of what to do.	*Give students options to present ideas in multiple ways. *Push students to go deeper with their connections, but be OK with students examining things more superficially.	*Use more sophisticated prompts that are closer to students' lived experiences. *Require more writing and deeper analysis of connections to the real world.

Adaptation for Different Assets and Needs

Time	
Limited Time	***Lots of Time***
*Keep the opening activities short and to the point. *Highlight students' voices daily to start class, but limit the number of students from day to day while trying to hear as many voices as possible during the remainder of the lesson.	*Take more time for both the opening activity and to highlight multiple new voices to start class each day. *Plan and integrate activities in the heart of the lesson that directly build on the students' voices at the start of class.
Diversity of Backgrounds	
Limited Diversity	***Lots of Diversity***
*Learn about students' backgrounds and make connections to students' lived experiences in your class' opening activities. You may discover more diversity than initially surmised. *Introduce new concepts, ideas, themes, and backgrounds during opening activities and facilitate dialogue that creates an open, safe, and inclusive space.	*Ensure all voices and backgrounds are heard and celebrated consistently rather than hearing the same voices daily. *Integrate students' backgrounds and diversity meaningfully into the curriculum. *Take extra time to create and maintain a safe, caring, supportive, and inclusive classroom setting.

STRATEGY 12: WORKING THE ROOM

> Teacher Contributors
> Jennifer Podolak Cline, Lawrence Middle School (NJ), 7th–8th grades
> Mary Eldredge-Sandbo, Des-Lacs Burlington High School (ND), 10th–12th grades

Working the room is the practice of reaching and connecting with all students by using the physical space of the classroom. It is a way of "taking the temperature" of the room to ensure that students are engaged throughout the lesson. This requires specific actions from the teacher at various points during the lesson that are made possible by the physical attributes of the classroom itself. Because each class has a different dynamic, working the room will look different in each and every classroom and with each and every class.

Strategy Implementation

1. **Greet students by name.** Greet each student by name as they enter the classroom. You may do this by standing at the door or from inside your classroom. Be sure to make eye contact with each student and say their name (correctly) as you greet them while also taking note of their disposition and demeanor to determine which students to prioritize quick check-ins with.

2. **Transition into the lesson with quick check-ins.** After greeting them, use the time before class begins to cultivate and maintain personal connections with students. Look for opportunities to just chat with students and learn about their interests, struggles, plans, etc. This can be as students get settled at their desks/tables or during the warmup activities. A simple, "how are you doing?" or specific check-in about something meaningful to the student will make a huge difference. To make these check-ins possible, be sure to circulate throughout the room to touch base with each student; it is a great way to simultaneously take attendance and connect with students. (See *Strategy 10: Check-Ins* for more on this.)

> **Get Yourself Ready to Work the Room!**
>
> As Jennifer Podolak Cline suggests, get yourself as the teacher ready to work the room each day:
> - Get yourself right before addressing kids; work hard behind the scenes before class starts so you can be truly present with each and every student.
> - Once the students enter the room, you're no longer the hardest worker in the room. You facilitate and coach; you're not the player.
>
> If something goes wrong while working the room, do tactical breathing to reset, and then focus on meeting the needs of your students.

3. **Establish and maintain beginning of class routines.** Set up a routine to start class that allows students to feel welcomed and seen, as well as space for you to connect with students. For example, play a Song of the Day as students take their seats and get ready for the warmup activity; then, as students get settled, circulate and check in with students who you noticed a need to touch base with during your greeting, students who have been absent, or students who just need a friendly smile. By keeping to the routine, students come to expect time and space to get settled, get to work, and have someone to see how they are doing and what they need.

> This past year, COVID-19 practices required that I wash each table between classes. I could have assigned students to do this, but I chose to do this task at the very beginning of class before students set their books down on the table. As I walked from table to table with my cloth and spray bottle, I could do quick check-ins with each student. Other opportunities for these conversations arise when walking down the hallway, during games, between classes, etc.
>
> —*Mary Eldredge-Sandbo*

4. **Arrange the room for collaboration, conversation, and movement.** There are many ways to arrange your room to maximize collaboration, conversation, and movement. Things to consider include:
    - *Desk or Table Configuration:* Based on the size and shape of your room, the types of tables or desks you have, and the number of students, determine a set-up that allows for easy circulation as well as shifting desks or tables from the original configuration to new ones based on changing collaboration needs.
    - *Number of Students:* Be cognizant of how best to set up your space based on your class size. With a small class, you can create seating that is more intimate while also having the space to give students their own space for independent work. For larger classes, be strategic with your room arrangement where there is little room for movement or changing the seating to maximize collaboration; be creative with desk or table placement and consider doing table clusters of groups, which typically allows for easier mobility and collaboration with larger classes.

> **Possible Desk or Table Configurations**
>
> - U-shape
> - Circle of individual desks or clumps of tables
> - Rows of desks or tables that can easily be moved into groups
> - Clumps of tables or desk groups scattered around the room

> I have tables in my room. We usually have some sort of set arrangement that is the result of my preference and theirs: I usually prefer groups of tables; students usually prefer rows. The tables have wheels, so I have students move the tables around so there are opportunities for different groups and various interactions. Even though students do choose where they sit, I mix things up for short periods of time so that they have the opportunity to collaborate with others in the classroom on a regular basis.
>
> —*Mary Eldredge-Sandbo*

- *Student Groupings:* Think about the types of groups you need for your class and then ensure your room set-up enables you to create those groups with the easiest possible transition. Are you constantly switching up groups or keeping the same groups for long periods of time? Are your groups larger or smaller or a combination? This will dictate how you arrange your room.
- *Take Notes:* As the teacher, while you navigate the room, take notes on the needs of students so you can circle back to your students' individual needs.

5. **Proximity matters, so keep moving.** While teaching, even during mini-lessons or interactive lectures, move around the room with purpose. Some tips include:
   - *Walk AWAY from Students to Get Them to Project:* When you call on a student, walk *away* from them to the other side of the room. (This goes against most people's natural inclination to walk toward the person with whom they are speaking.) Students typically just talk to the teacher, and by moving away, you encourage students to project their voice so you (and the rest of the class) can hear them. Additionally, because they will be looking at you, if you are across the room, it will have the appearance of them looking at the whole class and create a more inclusive dialogue.
   - *Use the Perimeter:* Use the perimeter of your classroom to deliver content, making a horseshoe pattern as you walk around the room, so you can monitor how each student is doing during the lesson.

> **Constantly Work the Room!**
>
> With a focus on the physical classroom and connecting with each student, routines, classroom arrangement, movement during class, and chances for conversations are all important tools that can easily be incorporated into daily instruction.
>
> —Mary Eldredge-Sandbo

Question Prompts for Groups While Working the Room

Check in with each group of students and go beyond the broad, "Any questions?" Instead, say to students:

- "Prove to me you understand _____."
- "What questions are coming up for you?"
- "Explain this to me."
- "Why are you doing this?"
- "What do you think will happen next? Why?"
- "What's not working? Why?"

Try to get a variety of answers from students in groups from *multiple* students and then follow up with written reflections with the same questions, giving students time to process and write their reflections on the group work.

> **Stand Back and Watch the Magic Happen**
>
> Sometimes just stand back and watch things happen. It's magical to stand back and watch and see if students are processing and engaged or if they are trying to figure something out and they're lost. If I notice they're lost, I might walk over or make a mental note to follow up later. Don't make a big thing about the errors, but follow up.
>
> —*Mary Eldredge-Sandbo*

- *Connect with Everyone:* When students are working at their tables or desks, in groups or individually, move around the room and connect with each student and group.
  - NOTE: When doing group work, once students start working, quickly touch base with *each* group to reinforce that they are getting off to a good start, and if a group needs help, give them one small thing to work on and let them know that you will return to them once you quickly check with everyone else. This ensures every student and group feels seen and supported from the outset of the activity.
- *See the Room:* Position your body and use your peripheral vision to see the entire room when working with a particular student.
- *Get on Students' Level:* If possible, kneel down next to the student's table so you're at eye level with them or sit on a chair beside them; do this while respecting their personal space.
- *Body Positioning:* Make sure you never have your back to the class. When kneeling to work with a student or group, position your body next to that student or group so you can still see the rest of the class to notice students who need help or just some acknowledgment.
- *Proximity:* Proximity is key to working the room; the physically closer you are to your students, the more likely they are to stay on task.

> **Never Turn Your Back!**
>
> In theater, actors are told never to turn their backs to the audience, and the same is true in the classroom: Teachers should rarely turn their backs to students. Keeping my gaze open while traveling to each group helps me to monitor students in my periphery.
>
> —*Jennifer Podolak Cline*

6. **Make the learning visual.** Provide students with opportunities and resources to make their learning visual through sharing and posting writing, drawings, brainstorms and other visual representations of learning and thinking. (For more on this, see *Strategy 18: Encouraging Students to Share Their Thinking and Feelings*.)
   - *Technology:* If you have technology available like laptops or tablets, integrate activities into your classroom where students can *post* work to shared platforms (like Jamboard, Padlet, or Google Slides).

- This allows for you and the rest of the class to collaborate in a more virtual environment and for students to still get individualized attention.
- While students work with their technology, you can move around the classroom to check-in with them in addition to checking their work digitally.
- *Physical Classroom:* Create spaces throughout your classroom where students can create and post their work (e.g., walls, desks, screens, etc.). This practice allows you to immediately see what students are thinking, learning, and processing. Just as important, it allows students to learn from and with each other and to take ownership of what they post on the boards. These visuals also provide a way for you to walk around the room, ask questions, and dig a bit deeper to learn about your students' learning. Examples include:
  - *Walls:* Create spaces on your classroom walls for students to post and comment on one another's work.
  - *Large Paper on Tables:* Use large paper on tables for students to collaborate on visual work that can later be hung up on the classroom wall or in the hallway.
  - *Desks:* With black science desks or other desks with tops that allow for writing, students can use neon markers or any washable marker to write and draw on their desks.
  - *Individual Whiteboards:* Each student can use their whiteboard to share their work.

7. **Use the whole room.** After delivering content, use the physical space in the classroom as much as possible. This could mean referencing/revisiting unit questions or big ideas on a bulletin board, soliciting student responses by using whiteboards (either on the wall or by using small, individual boards), having students navigate various learning stations, or students moving to different areas of the room with or without their desks for partner or independent work.

8. **System for getting the teacher's attention.** Establish a system for students to get your attention if they need assistance during the lesson. This can be something you determine *with* your students so they have buy-in to use the routine. Some techniques include:
   - *Green and Red Index Cards:* Give each student a green and red index card, folded in half to be hung on their desk. If a student has no questions, they put the green card on top and continue working independently. When they have a question or need help, they write a note on the red card and put that on top, and move on to another task until you have time to address their concern. As you circulate the room, put the date on their red card to track which students you have reached.
   - *Electronic Device Chats:* If working on an electronic device, you can use the chat function or direct messaging so students can privately ask for help.

STRATEGY IN ACTION: USING THE ENTIRE CLASSROOM—NAVIGATING GROUP WORK IN THE CLASSROOM SPACE

I was teaching advanced biology—a class with about 24 students in grades 11 and 12. We were just starting a project that the whole class would carry out, and we needed to agree on one plan—a model that would show a sustainable gathering place in a city. (This was part of a project to implement one Sustainable Development [SD] Goal).

Students were placed in groups depending on the work they chose to contribute to the project—research, construction, organization, documentation, etc. Students understood the SD goal they were working on, and they had already agreed on some criteria for their final project. What they couldn't decide on were the details for their gathering place.

I gave each group (about six groups) a handful of colored markers and sent them to a specific place in the room. I asked them to come up with a proposal that would meet the criteria, be feasible in terms of resources, and be "doable" according to our timeline. Students had about 30 minutes to draw, list, outline, etc. on their designated whiteboards. After that time, each group explained their work. Throughout this time, students stayed at their spots—standing or sitting.

While working, each group was very focused on their task; there was great and constructive conversation and a building of consensus as they worked. Students also listened attentively to each group's presentation. The next day, the same groups went to each section of the classroom and made notes and designations of the factors they thought were most important to include in the project. As a whole class, the students came up with a plan for how the model would come together.

We continued to use the boards for lists, progress notes, reminders, etc. It was amazing to see that some of the really "far out" ideas worked beautifully. Everyone had a say in the final product, and each group's proposal could be seen (in some capacity) in the final project.

The important things were that the students trusted each other enough to share their ideas and to build on each other's contributions. By moving, drawing, and talking with each other in the classroom, they were able to build that understanding more quickly and effectively.

As the project progressed, we routinely moved the tables into reasonable configurations so that each group could do the necessary work for the day. I loved the fact that the students were able to shift roles and move to different groups as needed. They were all proud of the final project, and as they did the work, they were building content knowledge.

—*Mary Eldredge-Sandbo*

STRATEGY IN ACTION: CONNECTING WITH EACH STUDENT FOR THE GOOD OF THE WHOLE CLASS

After 14 years of teaching in three different school districts, one thing remains true: middle school students want to be heard, and they need a safe space in order for them to express themselves. In order to create this safe space, remind yourself that your classroom isn't yours, it's theirs. In the walls of your shared space, students should feel seen, heard, and inspired to shine.

Often this means diverting from your perfectly planned lesson to meet students where they are. I'll never forget the day after Kobe Bryant died. One of my students—we'll call him Connor—was absolutely devastated. He didn't have to tell me how he felt with words, his grief was controlling his hunched body as he tried to make himself as small as possible entering my classroom. This was the complete opposite of his normal gregarious and outgoing behavior.

After reading the directions for the bellringer activity, I approached his desk and asked what was going on. He told me he was really upset that his hero had died, but additionally, he was mad his parents forced him to go to school in spite of his emotional pain.

Instead of completing whatever bellringer activity I had assigned, I asked him to take out his Writer's Notebook and write a letter to Kobe. His posture immediately changed, and he looked at me and said, "Really?" to which I replied, "Really."

Connor then spent the next 10 minutes writing his letter. After time was called, I asked if he was ready and willing to join class, and he nodded and told me he felt much better.

Had I ignored Connor—or worse, told him to move on or stop acting sad—I would have done more damage than good. Working the room really boils down to your connections with each student for the good of the whole class. It means meeting your students where they are, making space for each one of them, and showing your students again and again that they truly matter to you.

—*Jennifer Podolak Cline*

How to Implement the Strategy at Varied Grade Levels

Elementary	*Middle*	*High*
*Visit with students in reading corners, playtime spaces, and other areas. *Focus on being a positive energy in the room and touching base with students.	*Be cognizant of everything they are going through in terms of their physical, emotional, and psychological development when doing check-ins, setting up table groups, etc.	*Honor students' sense of becoming adults and needing some independence when considering how you touch base with them and use your physical classroom space.

> **Not Your Room? No Problem!**
>
> If you are a *traveling* teacher who moves from room to room, you can still work the room. Some tips to make this work include:
>
> - Move the students more than the furniture.
> - Create smaller groups that are more mobile.
> - Have students *start class* by changing the physical room to your needs and then *end class* by returning the classroom to its previous configuration.

Considering Different Types of Learners

Though each of the adaptations are likely to benefit all students, the "X" marks indicate adaptations to this strategy that are particularly helpful for English-language learners, Special Education students, and Gifted and Talented students.

		English-Language Learners		
Provide visuals	Label materials in multiple languages	Translate instructions/ materials to their primary language	Model expectations/ processes	Invite students to write/speak in primary language
		X	X	X
		Special Education Students		
Scaffold instructions/ chunking	Provide positive reinforcement	Schedule breaks	Offer multiple options/formats for student to choose	Minimize distractions
X	X			X
		Gifted and Talented Students		
Encourage students to focus on learning rather than grades	Celebrate nonacademic successes with students	Provide opportunities for students to take individualized ownership of learning	Challenge students to use more sophisticated vocabulary	Invite students to share how their thinking is extended by hearing new perspectives
X	X			

Adaptation for Different Assets and Needs

Academic Diversity	
Limited Diversity	*Lots of Diversity*
*Remember, things may look the same, but students always have individualized needs when it comes to learning.	*Ensure that you are individualizing your check-ins with students based on what you know about their academic strengths and needs.
*If you teach multiple classes/sections, change up how you work the room from class to class based on students' strengths and needs.	*Normalize checking in with all students regardless of their academic strengths and needs.

Physical Size of Classroom	
Small Classroom	*Large Classroom*
*Play with the room configuration to ensure there is ample room for you to navigate the room easily and for students to move into different groupings.	*Create many different work spaces that can be used to support student learning in a variety of ways.
*Create interactive spaces using bulletin boards or digital platforms like Jamboard where students can share and you can respond.	*Prioritize movement around the room on a daily basis.

WHY I LIKE THIS STRATEGY

By working the room, teachers demonstrate that their classroom is student-centered and that each student matters; determine the emotional state of students and address any nonacademic needs; provide opportunities for student struggle, questions, and feedback; and gauge the effectiveness of a lesson, activity, strategy, etc.

—*Jennifer Podolak Cline*

Classroom movement and arrangement, once trust is established, can take connecting with students to a different level. One of my favorite things is when we realize that something just isn't making sense to one or more students, and we can work together to figure out how to work through it. Just small opportunities for movement can make a big difference. Asking students to go to the whiteboard cupboards for a quick activity provides the time for them to get out of their chair, adjust their thinking, see the room differently, and get back to work. Sometimes, we just move for the sake of moving—get up and stretch for 30 seconds.

—*Mary Eldredge-Sandbo*

STRATEGY 13: BRAIN AND BODY BREAKS

> Teacher Contributors
> *Alyssa Landy, Luria Academy (NY), 4th–5th grades*
> *Pamela Goff, Hedgepeth-Williams Middle School (NJ), 7th grade*

Brain and body breaks are an opportunity for teachers and students to reset their brains and bodies. These breaks are aimed at helping everyone reengage and focus during a school day that is often physically, emotionally, and psychologically draining. Breaks can be integrated into the daily routine as well as done on an as-needed basis for the entire class, small groups, or individuals.

Strategy Implementation

1. **Develop a stockpile of breaks to use.** There are many types of breaks that can benefit your students. Have a stockpile of breaks to either help ground or energize them! Remember, when doing energizing breaks, take a moment at the end to help students ground and reengage with what they were doing or are about to do.
   - *Brain:* Sometimes students need a chance to relax their brains if they have been overly stressed or to energize their brains if they are bored. Examples of grounding and energizing brain breaks include:
     - Grounding
       - *Reading:* Give everyone a chance to quietly read something that interests them for a short period of time before returning to your content.
       - *Calming Visuals:* Watch a calming video together. Platforms like *GoNoodle* provide great options.
       - *Mindfulness-Based Breathing:* Guide the class through breathing exercises that help center the students, calm their brains, and get to a point where they are ready to return to learning. (See *Strategy 14: Mindfulness* for more on mindfulness approaches.)
     - Energizing
       - *Simon Says:* This kids game really works for all ages! To play, a "leader" says to the group, "Simon says" and then they do an action like touching their nose. They keep doing this and sometimes do it without saying "Simon says." If anyone does the action when the leader does not say "Simon says," they are eliminated. Consider having a student be the leader.
       - *Distraction:* If students are stressed out, distract them with something they *really like* (e.g., If they love animals, distract them with pictures of puppies; if they like jokes, look up jokes.). This allows for some of the intensity of that emotion to diminish, so they can address what is causing that stress.
       - *Drumming:* Give a student who needs help focusing a drum they can beat every time they hear an important point. Students can take turns being in charge of the drum.
       - *Four Corners:* Ask the whole class a question that has four possible answers (e.g., strongly agree, somewhat agree, somewhat disagree,

strongly disagree); then have them move to a corner of the room based on their answers. Students can then talk with other students who had the same answer and then discuss as a class. Repeat as many times as needed.
- *Would You Rather?* Ask students a question with two answers and have them stand up or sit down based on which answer they prefer. Discuss and then repeat. (Teaching virtually? This can work with having students turn their cameras on or off based on their preferred answer.)
- *Brain Gym:* This book by Dennison and Dennison (1994), and their accompanying videos and online activities, provide movement-based brain activities.

> Sometimes the brain or body break method you've chosen just doesn't work and you try not to get frustrated. Step back, reevaluate, and think of other options you can use and adjust your practice as quickly as possible.
>
> —Alyssa Landy

- *Body:* Students typically spend most of the school day sitting, which has different effects on different students. Some students get restless and need grounding; others get lethargic and need energizing. Examples of grounding and energizing body breaks include:
  ◦ Grounding
    - *Yoga:* Practice yoga poses that can be done next to seats, in open spaces in the classroom, or in the hallway.
    - *Stretching:* Do stretches for both the upper and lower body.
    - *Lemon Squeeze:* Squeeze your whole body like biting into a sour lemon, then breathe out.
    - *Trace Hand while Taking Deep Breaths:* You can do this while breathing at your own pace or by doing box breathes where you count three seconds to breathe in, hold your breath for three seconds, and then breathe out for three seconds.
    - *Go for a Walk:* This can include giving students a task like taking a note to another teacher. NOTE: This is not punitive; sometimes students just need to move!
  ◦ Energizing
    - *Hopscotch:* Set up hopscotch using tape on the ground in your classroom or in the hallways where students can skip and jump and play for a few minutes before returning back to learning.
    - *Fidgets:* For students who need to be doing something, have fidgets like beads on a string that they can play with, even while learning is continuing.
    - *Hands Partner Game:* Pair students and have them stand up and face each other. Then have one student hold their hands up in fists and the other person holds their hands in front of the other person with open hands. Then, they need to watch each other, and switch opening and closing their hands so one person always has fists and one person always has open hands.
    - *Calisthenics:* Have students do something active while standing in place. This can include doing jumping jacks, jogging in place, or spinning in a circle.

> **Why Brain and Body Breaks Are So Important!**
>
> - Students can focus on their work.
> - Students' moods are more evened out.
> - Sometimes it lifts energy up, sometimes it calms students.

> **Generate Brain and Body Break Buy-In!**
>
> - Do the exercises *with* the students.
> - Make it fun, and let reticent students see how fun it is.
> - Explain research that tells students how breaks are good for your brains and muscles and makes you calmer and less stressed.

- *Individual versus Collaborative:* When engaging in breaks, determine whether the break should be done together or alone.
    - *Individual:* Use individualized breaks when students need to work on centering or reengaging themselves and when collaborative breaks might lead to greater distractions.
    - *Collaborative:* Use collaborative or group breaks when students need to feed off one another's energy to help ground or get energized.

2. **When.** It is important to determine when brain and body breaks are needed. It is useful to integrate these breaks into your daily routine and to note signs that indicate certain breaks are needed for individuals, groups, or the entire class.
    - *Daily Routine:* Find a time that works to build in brain and body breaks daily. It's often helpful to include these breaks as part of *transitions*:
        - *Into Your Classroom:* Before diving into any of your content for the day, take a moment to ground together and get ready for your time together.
        - *Between Activities or Content Areas:* When transitioning between activities for your lesson, shifting content areas in elementary school, or moving from group work to independent work, build in a brain or body break to serve as a means to help students reset and get ready for their next endeavor.

        > Take the pulse of the kids and yourself and ask, "do we need a break and is it a good time for a break?"
        >
        > —Pamela Goff

        - *Out of Your Classroom:* When students are going to leave your classroom for their next class, lunch, or recess, engage in a meaningful brain or body break to get them settled and ready for the change.

> **Share Break Ideas with Colleagues!**
>
> Everyone should use them! Keep a shared notebook of brain and body breaks. Create opportunities to teach them to each other in-person. This can help teachers who don't use breaks see their importance and understand how they can use them in their classroom. This sharing also gives teachers who already use them a chance to share and steal great breaks from one another!
>
> *—Pamela Goff*

- *Whole-Class Indicators:* Pay attention to the mood, posture, affect, or general nature of the class. If the class is unfocused, consider:
    - Are they wiggly or distracted by friends? If so, do a quick grounding break to help them become more centered and focused.
    - Are they bored, zoning out, and slouching in their seats? If so, do a quick energizing break.
    - Pause whatever you are doing for a brain or body break and then transition back into whatever you were doing.
- *Small Group Indicators:* When your students are engaged in group work, as you work the room and connect with each group, pay attention to whether particular groups need a quick break to reset and reengage in their work.
- *Individual Indicators:* Try to see each student throughout your class and notice any signs that they need a quick break. If a student is distracted, extremely hyper, or unusually quiet, try the following:
    - Help the students figure out what type of break they need and why they need it. Ultimately, help students learn to take action to address their needs on their own.
    - For students that need to consistently take individual breaks, consider making a goals chart where they can self-assess and determine when and what kind of break they need to take.

Considering Different Types of Learners

Though each of the adaptations are likely to benefit all students, the "X" marks indicate adaptations to this strategy that are particularly helpful for English-language learners, Special Education students, and Gifted and Talented students.

English-Language Learners				
Provide visuals	Label materials in multiple languages	Translate instructions/ materials to their primary language	Model expectations/ processes	Invite students to write/speak in primary language
X		X	X	X
Special Education Students				
Scaffold instructions/ chunking	Provide positive reinforcement	Schedule breaks	Offer multiple options/formats for student to choose	Minimize distractions
X	X		X	X
Gifted and Talented Students				
Encourage students to focus on learning rather than grades	Celebrate nonacademic successes with students	Provide opportunities for students to take individualized ownership of learning	Challenge students to use more sophisticated vocabulary	Invite students to share how their thinking is extended by hearing new perspectives
X	X			X

How to Implement the Strategy at Varied Grade Levels

Elementary	Middle	High
*Make it extra fun and simple at first. Then build up to more challenging types of breaks. *Build breaks into multiple transitions throughout the day while also being flexible to take breaks whenever you notice a need.	*Be mindful of students' transition into and out of your class/lessons and try to do short breaks during both of these transitions. *Take turns leading the breaks with the students.	*Set up a system for students to signal the need for breaks. *Let students take more ownership of leading the breaks.

WHY I LIKE THIS STRATEGY

Children require opportunities to reset and shift their focus in order to reengage their minds and bodies.

—*Alyssa Landy*

Brain and body breaks are great because they help you step away from the curriculum and help students increase their focus and energy. You have to keep things light and allow them to be kids! They need to feel comfortable; there are going to be kids who want to sit down; they want to sit it out, but you encourage them to stand up and stretch, move, and breathe. We're not going to sit for 80 minutes—we need to move. Students need to be able to be kids and have conversations and laugh.

—*Pamela Goff*

Adaptation for Different Assets and Needs

Class Size	
Small Class	**Large Class**
*Allow students to take more ownership leading the breaks.	*Move activities into the hallway or other spaces outside of your classroom.
*Have a balance of whole-class, group, and individual breaks built into your class.	*Do more whole-class breaks than group or individual.

Time	
Limited Time	**Lots of Time**
*Do quicker breaks.	*Build breaks into your routine, ensuring there is a break in the middle of your class.
*Focus on including breaks at the beginning and end of class, and sprinkle in breaks in the middle when necessary.	*Integrate multiple breaks daily, some planned and some spontaneous.

STRATEGY IN ACTION: READING THE ROOM FOR BRAIN AND BODY BREAKS

One morning, I walked into the classroom ready to start my lesson. My students were in a class with another teacher prior to my arrival and the class seemed a bit chaotic. I was about to start my "Do Now" when I overheard one of my students making lots of noises. I knew it was an indicator of some type of stress. Usually, I would offer up a private body break for this student (he does well when he leaves the space for a few minutes of movement). However, I realized that since it was a transition, that all of the kids could benefit from a calming body and brain break. I had them stand up, we did a few yoga poses and ended with some mindful breathing. That one particular child who was making the noises, discontinued and was able to refocus his energy. In that moment, I realized how important it is to step back for a moment when you walk into chaos; you may find that something good for one, can be beneficial to all.

—*Alyssa Landy*

STRATEGY IN ACTION: BRAIN AND BODY BREAKS IN A MIDDLE SCHOOL MATH CLASS

Brain and body breaks in the classroom are really about timing. If students have been working in their spaces for a while, then getting them up and just having them do something physical reenergizes them.

I do a skip counting game in my math class where we go in the hallway and students stand with a partner. I give them a number to skip count back and forth to by adding multiples of that number. The counting works the brain because they're trying to skip count back and forth and have to communicate with each other. They get really into it and say, "Oh, can we do another number," and it's not really about avoiding work, but it's just because they're enjoying themselves.

That is the satisfying part of using any of those brain breaks—it's when they can say, "Oh, can we do that again? Can we pick the number?" And so it's not just that they don't see it as an instructional strategy, it's that they are enjoying themselves, so let's continue that. Students are communicating with each other, and they love and need that.

Sometimes when I lead these breaks, the students want to take over leading the break for the class. Then, once they start, they begin imitating me, and I just can't help but crack up because they're doing the work of it, but they are imitating me for some comedic effect, and it's hilarious. We all laugh. Laughter is so important in the classroom and is a needed break for everyone!

—*Pamela Goff*

STRATEGY 14: MINDFULNESS

> Teacher Contributors
> Anthony Tumolo, Readington Township Public Schools (NJ),
> Kindergarten–8th grades
> Thomas (TJ) Belasco, Lower Cape May Regional High School (NJ),
> 9th–12th grades

Mindfulness helps students and teachers build competency in self-awareness and self-management. Self-awareness is the ability to identify personal feelings and perceptions. When a person is self-aware, they can tap into their emotions (e.g., embarrassment) and note the sensations (e.g., cheeks getting hot) that accompany that emotion. This awareness supports self-management, pausing to decide how to respond to a situation rather than having emotion drive a reaction. Mindfulness practices to build self-awareness and self-management include breathing exercises, visualization, and physical movement such as yoga.

> Social Emotional Learning supports academics. It's not a separate thing—it's what we do.
>
> —Anthony Tumolo

Strategy Implementation

1. **Determine *why* you want to use mindfulness.** Consider your reasons for implementing mindfulness in your classroom. Ask yourself:
   - Are you trying to help an anxious class?
   - Is this something you want to try with specific students or the whole class?

   Use the answers to your *why* questions to guide *how* and *when* you implement mindfulness in your classroom.

2. **Explore *how* to use mindfulness.** There are so many techniques available. Consider:
   - *Videos:* Watch mindfulness videos like the free K–12 curriculum at pureedgeinc.org
   - *Apps:* Try insight timer (free); Ten Percent Happier (Scholarships can be offered on a need basis); and Calm.
   - *Working with a Mindfulness Coach:* This might be an outside person who the district hires or a counselor or fellow teacher in your building.
   - *Use a Book:* Books like *I Am Peace* on page 93 or *Anytime Yoga* offer great mindfulness practices and advice.
   - See *Favorite Mindfulness Practices* on page 93 for many more options.

> Once you find a voice you like on any of the apps, look up as much of what they have available as possible. I find students all relate to different voices. The process is not a one-size fits all.
>
> —TJ Belasco

> Learn the techniques of getting out of your head. Stop the mind from perpetuating an exciting experience.
>
> —TJ Belasco

Favorite Mindfulness Practices

Mindful Breathing. Set the tone for class by engaging students in two minutes of mindful breathing. It serves to calm, ground, and focus the day.
- Explain that mindful breathing involves focusing awareness on what is happening in your body as you breathe.
- Show how to take a deep breath that fills the lungs and presses out the stomach. (Some people call this a *Buddha Breath*.)
- Practice together:
  - Breathe in for four seconds
  - Hold for seven seconds
  - Breathe out for eight seconds
- Every 20 seconds, give some guidance:
  - Focus awareness on the sensations in the lungs and stomach.
  - Encourage students to breathe in positive feelings and breathe out their stress.
  - Remind students that it's ok if thoughts are coming in. Acknowledge the thoughts, and return to awareness of the breath and the sensations in their body.
- After two minutes, give students 10 to 20 seconds to come back to the space and get ready for the day. This may mean opening their eyes if they were closed, wiggling toes and fingers, and rolling out their shoulders and neck. Build on that calm and focus with an engaging learning experience.

Walking Meditation. This is a good way to separate a student from a stressful situation and help them get grounded. To do this:
- Step away from the situation that is causing stress.
- Walk one lap around the school hallway.
- While walking, think about lifting your foot, carrying your foot forward, and placing your foot down—really feel contact with the ground with each step.

Five Things. This is an easy way to help students pause and take in their surroundings. Think of:
- Five things you can see
- Four things you can hear
- Three things you can touch
- Two things you can smell
- One thing you can taste (consider keeping a bag of mints on your desk for this)

Come Back to Calm. In the Readington Township District, Come Back to Calm means taking a moment for students to pause and slow down. When a teacher asks students to Come Back to Calm, students:
- Pause what they are doing,
- Put a hand on their heart,

- Put a hand on their belly, and
- Take three breaths.

Come Back to Calm encourages students to take the time to make a decision about how to respond to physical experiences or emotions in our bodies, thus supporting more of a thoughtful response than an emotional reaction.

—Anthony Tumolo

Affirmations. Through affirmations, students and teachers can remind themselves of the character traits they want to embody. Affirmations work by using the following steps:
- Build affirmations around character traits you want to support. For example, if the character trait is *responsibility*, the affirmation may be "I am responsible for my words, actions, and thoughts" (affirmations represent the desired results).
- Encourage students to consider how they can embody the trait and the related affirmation. For example, discuss how students are responsible for themselves at each grade level and in each content area.
- Encourage teachers to consider how they teach the character trait and support the affirmation. For example, how do I teach responsibility through my content area (reading, math, science)?
- Check in to see how well you are living your affirmation. For example, at the end of the month or end of the marking period, ask students to share stories of how they lived their affirmations in and out of class.

3. **Consider *when* to use mindfulness.** Think about when it makes sense to use mindfulness with your students. Some possible times where mindfulness will be impactful include:
   - Starting class with grounding and focused breathing.
   - Getting wiggles out through yoga after recess.
   - Engaging in a sensory activity to calm the mind before a test or experience that requires a lot of focus.
   - Pausing to do a body scan before reacting to a situation.

4. **Build trust.** Students have a great radar for teachers who are trying to be something other than who they are. Be honest about being new to this or being uncomfortable or nervous. If you are doing something that involves closing eyes, let students have the choice of closing their eyes or looking at a spot on the floor. Let them know that you are not judging how they participate.

> Mindfulness practice is an investment in education. More importantly, it's an investment in these kids understanding themselves.
>
> —TJ Belasco

5. **Start small.** Meditation, focused breathing, and yoga take time and focus. It makes sense to start small. When students are engaged in a breathing exercise for 2 minutes, it can feel like 30 minutes. Start small and build up to longer experiences.

6. **Emphasize it's ok to struggle with mindfulness.** Mindfulness is a practice. When you practice, you are going to have good days and not-so-good days. Compare getting distracted during mindfulness with when you are sitting and reading a book but you don't know what you read. You realize that you weren't paying attention. That's the nature of being human. When you realize that, you become better at being more present.

7. **Encourage student ownership.** As students become more comfortable with mindfulness practices, encourage them to lead the class. This can be added to your list of class jobs (see *Strategy 9: Classroom Jobs*.)

Considering Different Types of Learners

Though each of the adaptations are likely to benefit all students, the "X" marks indicate adaptations to this strategy that are particularly helpful for English-language learners, Special Education students, and Gifted and Talented students.

		English-Language Learners		
Provide visuals	Label materials in multiple languages	Translate instructions/ materials to their primary language	Model expectations/ processes	Invite students to write/speak in primary language
X		X	X	
		Special Education Students		
Scaffold instructions/ chunking	Provide positive reinforcement	Schedule breaks	Offer multiple options/formats for student to choose	Minimize distractions
X	X		X	X
		Gifted and Talented Students		
Encourage students to focus on learning rather than grades	Celebrate nonacademic successes with students	Provide opportunities for students to take individualized ownership of learning	Challenge students to use more sophisticated vocabulary	Invite students to share how their thinking is extended by hearing new perspectives
X	X			

How to Implement the Strategy at Varied Grade Levels

Elementary	Middle	High
*Connect with your school's social emotional learning curriculum. *Keep it short and sweet. Breathing exercises or yoga can be as little as one minute.	*Offer options and let students choose mindfulness practices that work for them. *Because middle school is a time when adolescents are dealing with shifts in hormones and social changes, practicing mindfulness is especially important. Be ready to give frequent reminders of options to pause and prepare for a response rather than a reaction by engaging in mindfulness practices.	*If students have been practicing mindfulness throughout their years in school, build on this. Find out what has worked well for them, and explore new practices together. *Encourage students to practice mindfulness outside of school. This might be something they do if they are getting stressed or have a conflict at work or home and need to pause before responding.

WHY I LIKE THIS STRATEGY

Your breath is the basis of all other exercises. So, a solid foundation in breathwork guides you throughout all forms of mindfulness. Additionally, each breath serves as the perfect reminder of leaving the past and not fixating on the future. Just *be here now*.

—*TJ Belasco*

Mindfulness teaches individuals to pay attention to their physical and emotional body. It helps young people identify and manage their physical and emotional sensations and feelings in order to help them make responsible decisions rooted in respect and kindness. It also teaches people to pause and come into the breath, which allows the mind and body to recenter and build present awareness. All of these benefits support learning, personal growth, and health and well-being.

—*Anthony Tumolo*

STRATEGY IN ACTION: LOVING KINDNESS PRACTICE

I am the Social and Emotional Learning (SEL) Supervisor for my district. There are four school buildings I serve. I work very closely with the building principals and school counselors throughout the year. One of the programs we created to support SEL integration is the creation of monthly SEL assemblies. A key portion of these gatherings is a teacher-led mindfulness practice centered around a character theme.

Last year, I guided the entire staff and students through the Loving Kindness Practice. The students and adults were asked to find a comfortable seat and softly close their eyes if that feels good to them. We took three deep breaths to create present awareness. Then the participants were asked to think about a person or people in their life who they care about deeply. They were asked to repeat the following in their minds to send them a bit of kindness:

1. May you be happy.
2. May you be healthy.
3. May you be peaceful.
4. May you be filled with joy.

We repeated this two more times, one where we sent the message to everyone around us and finally to ourselves by replacing the word *you* with *I*.

The response to this practice was overwhelmingly positive. Students and adults shared that they felt uplifted, joyful, and rejuvenated. Some reported they even practiced this strategy on their own when they were feeling sad or when they felt others needed some positive energy.

We learned that there is true power in sending joy to ourselves and others. We also found that this practice helps to build empathy and compassion, especially when we send this message to someone we may disagree with. Teachers and caregivers shared that we are all human beings who deserve happiness, health, and peace.

—Anthony Tumolo

Adaptation for Different Assets and Needs

Buy-In	
Skeptical about Mindfulness *Use terminology that doesn't refer directly to mindfulness (e.g., *breathing exercises* to start class). *In your school, encourage colleagues to let go of skepticism and expectations that students already know how to manage their emotions. It is up to teachers to guide and reinforce emotional regulation skills with students.	**Open to Mindfulness** *Maintain a consistent practice in your classroom. *In your school, build the language to have conversations about the impact of mindfulness.

Time	
Limited Time *Remember, even a little time goes a long way. Just one minute of mindfulness will be a positive time investment for the rest of the day. *Build a short mindfulness exercise into your opening or closing to your lesson.	**Lots of Time** *Work up to longer sessions. *Incorporate varied practices. *Integrate mindfulness into your class's daily practice.

STRATEGY IN ACTION: BREATHING

The mindfulness practices that started as a way to set the tone and mood for our class period have spread throughout the school. Students created an after-school club, *Mindfulness Over Matter*; I now lead a weekly morning practice for teachers, some of whom have brought mindfulness into their classroom; and coaches have reached out to me to share mindfulness techniques with their teams.

Perhaps the truest test of this practice was related back to me by one of my students. One of my favorite techniques is one I picked up from Max Strom that I believe was originally taught by Andrew Weil. This consists of a simple 4-7-8 breathing pattern. Breath in for four seconds, hold for seven seconds, and exhale for eight seconds. As our breathing is so connected to our parasympathetic nervous system, this simple activity done 6 to 8 times helps regulate emotion and calm students down.

My best example of this was a few weeks after we had done this activity together at the start of a class, I had a student who said he was becoming annoyed in his math class. Rather than leaving or acting out, he just closed his eyes and used the 4-7-8 activity. He was amazed by how much calmer he felt afterward. By no means perfect, but it was enough for him to handle the situation.

—*TJ Belasco*

STRATEGY 15: SPOTLIGHTING STUDENTS

> Teacher Contributors
> *Kate Sullivan, A. P. Willits Elementary School (NY), Kindergarten*
> *Janice Wilke, The Baldwin School (PA), 9th–12th grades*

Teachers often pause to "shout out" what they see students doing well. This can be something as simple as stating, "I like the way Surama has her book out and her notebook open." It can also be more involved, like having the class pause so that students in a group can share their process and product as a model for others. This strategy focuses on ways to integrate the practice of spotlighting students' work into your classroom routines. When students see what their peers are doing, they can better understand expectations, envision their own next steps, and engage in a classroom community that promotes support of one another.

Strategy Implementation

1. **Determine *how* to spotlight student work.** There are multiple ways you might share student work with your class. Based on your technology access, consider:
   - *High Tech*
     - Projecting the work on a screen in the front of the room.
     - Taking pictures of student work and sharing via slides.
     - Using a document camera.
   - *Low Tech*
     - Providing individual copies of student work to share with the class.
     - Having students gather around the work.

   > Something about students seeing their work on the screen in front of the whole class makes the work somehow more meaningful.
   > —Janice Wilke

2. **Decide *what* to spotlight.** Look for student work that will lead to the next *teachable moment*. (See *Strategy in Action: Student Profile* on page 102 for a model of spotlighting several aspects of an individual students' work each week.) Spotlight work that:
   - Accomplishes the goals of a lesson.
   - Shows students effectively implementing strategies.
   - Demonstrates new perspectives that arise.

3. **Create a culture of sharing.** Let students know that you intend to share their work. Be sure to:
   - *Invite Students to Share Work:* Tell students that you need help with modeling. Keep the language of this invitation simple. Make clear the skills you are looking to highlight and that you will choose different people at

   > The second you say to a child they are going to act like the teacher, you see a little spark in them.
   > —Kate Sullivan

different times. As they get used to this, they may *ask* to be spotlighted.
- *Get Students' Permission to Share:* Most students will be excited to have their work shared; however, if a student does not give permission, encourage them to share in the future. A "no" today may become a "yes" tomorrow, once the student sees how the process plays out.

> When you start highlighting students' work, it may be easier to begin with a few models from former students so the students get used to practicing positive feedback without the creator of the work in the room.
>
> —Kate Sullivan

- *Make Sharing Work Exciting:* Spotlighting students for the positive choices they make helps students celebrate small and big successes. Consider ways the class can show appreciation for the work that was shared. They might:
  - Snap or clap for the highlighted student.
  - Shout a class-created chant or cheer.
  - See *Strategy 3: Positive Affirmations* on pages 13–14.

4. **Facilitate dialogue.** Help students discuss the shared work in a positive, meaningful way. Frame this with:
   - *Feedback Sandwich:* Students start with a positive statement, then make a suggestion for growth, and end with another positive statement.
   - *Feedback Starters:* Post a list of sentence starters in the room. Share some examples and then ask students to add to the list. Possible feedback sentence starters include:
     - "I like how you . . ."
     - "This reminds me of . . ."
     - "Maybe you can add . . ."

5. **Be inclusive of all.** Keep track of which students you've highlighted and how you've talked about their work. Do your best to consistently spotlight students in little ways, and highlight each student over the course of the year in big ways, so all students feel part of this sharing community.

> I'm very aware of keeping the same format so students are treated equally with the spotlight.
>
> —Janice Wilke

6. **Save models.** It's a great idea to ask students if you can hold on to a picture of their work to show in the future. This has two benefits:
   - The student feels even more validated because their work is worth archiving.
   - You get a model to use in the future.

Considering Different Types of Learners

Though each of the adaptations are likely to benefit all students, the "X" marks indicate adaptations to this strategy that are particularly helpful for English-language learners, Special Education students, and Gifted and Talented students.

English-Language Learners				
Provide visuals	Label materials in multiple languages	Translate instructions/materials to their primary language	Model expectations/processes	Invite students to write/speak in primary language
X			X	
Special Education Students				
Scaffold instructions/chunking	Provide positive reinforcement	Schedule breaks	Offer multiple options/formats for student to choose	Minimize distractions
	X		X	X
Gifted and Talented Students				
Encourage students to focus on learning rather than grades	Celebrate nonacademic successes with students	Provide opportunities for students to take individualized ownership of learning	Challenge students to use more sophisticated vocabulary	Invite students to share how their thinking is extended by hearing new perspectives
X		X		X

How to Implement the Strategy at Varied Grade Levels

Elementary	Middle	High
*Use accessible language that makes spotlighting fun (e.g., "Today, I need a teacher's helper to show what [xxx] looks like."). *When students share, explicitly let them know what you like about their choices or ideas, which reinforces expectations.	*Remember this can be an age when students feel self-conscious, so be sure to get permission to share. *Be especially explicit about expectations around how to give positive feedback.	*Discuss the varied ways that students achieve success. This metacognitive focus will be important for students as they enter college and their career. *Give opportunities for students to lead the discussions.

STRATEGY IN ACTION: STUDENT PROFILE PAGES

My strategy to increase student engagement and confidence is to show, on the Smartboard in class, a teacher-created "profile page" of each student. This is my interpretation of what makes that particular student special and artistic in their own way. I concentrate on a few photos of the student and how they work, perhaps the organization of their palette or their posture at the easel, a few shots of their work in progress, a surprise picture of what I (as the more experienced visual artist) see as possible forebears or connections with their work, maybe a funny shot or two of untied sneakers or paint on the uniform, and something the student has said that has struck me.

I started using this strategy with a hyperactive middle school art elective class. Their "antics" were put in context with their achievements, creating a way to embrace the antics on my part, and a focus on the achievements for them. I tried it again with an advanced upper school painting class. Even the shyer students realized that their work could be a kind of initial stand-in for themselves; that expression goes beyond the loudest, the most easily articulated, or the most outrageous or well-balanced opinion in the room. The painters began to search for more individual responses as opposed to "finding an image on the internet and copying it." And, let's face it, everybody likes a bit of personal attention! I end the student highlight with a question, but the focus is positive; I do not highlight what still needs to be learned or the weaker aspects of a student's work.

—*Janice Wilke*

WHY I LIKE THIS STRATEGY

I like this strategy because it is a huge motivator for kindergarten students. (Who doesn't want to share their hard work on the Promethean board?!) Given the circumstances of the pandemic, our partner work/contact is much more limited than in years past. This allows the entire class to serve as a *partner* for the spotlighted student. It is also important to have the permission of the student so that they do not feel uncomfortable.

—*Kate Sullivan*

Students enjoy seeing themselves portrayed positively by the teacher, and I try to focus on individual qualities of the student. Everyone is different and that is what we are seeing and celebrating. Everyone's work has a good quality to be highlighted, no matter the skill level. Behavior, comportment, confidence, and class atmosphere improve dramatically.

—*Janice Wilke*

Adaptation for Different Assets and Needs

Class Size	
Small Class *Vary the ways you spotlight students because you will have the opportunity to do so more often. *Spotlight teachers, staff, and other adults who work in your classroom.	**Large Class** *Spotlight groups of students. *Develop a system for keeping spotlights short and powerful so you have more time to spotlight multiple students.

Time	
Limited Time *Remember that spotlighting student work can be something that happens in-the-moment or something that is scheduled. If you do this more in the moment, it is especially important to keep track of who you have highlighted so you make sure to spotlight students equally. *Commit to spotlighting a reasonable number of students over a set period of time. You might do this by counting how many weeks are in the marking period and mapping how many students you need to spotlight each week in order to give each student a boost.	**Lots of Time** *Set a time for weekly student spotlights. *Challenge yourself to spotlight students more often! Rather than once a marking period, make it two or three times a marking period. This means you will need to have a system for keeping track of when and why you have spotlighted each student.

STRATEGY IN ACTION: SHARING WORK INSTANTANEOUSLY

I first tried this spotlighting strategy during the 2020–2021 school year with my kindergarten students. Not knowing how it would work or how the students would react, I tried it on a whim. My document camera was not working, the desks were so spread out that few students would be able to see if I simply held up the work, and I had a brand new Promethean board that I was still learning how to use.

The students were working on three-page pattern books, using familiar spelling words to construct simple sentences (e.g., "I see the slide. I see the swing. I see the monkey bars.") and I needed a good example to share. I quickly went around the classroom and informally assessed their writing until I found a cute pattern book about Disney World. The student had written a pattern that I knew would engage the rest of the class ("I see the castle. I see the roller coaster. I see Mickey Mouse."), so I quickly took photos of each page using my iPhone and emailed them to myself. I uploaded the photos onto Google Slides, got the class's attention, and projected the images onto the board.

The class (and the student writer) lit up when they saw the writing. The student explained each page to us, discussing her pictures, labels, and sentences. I reminded the rest of the class about ways to compliment or make suggestions to our classmates. Out of 22 students, at least 20 had their hands up to participate. I started hearing comments like, "I like your castle picture, but I think you should add an exclamation point!" or "You wrote so neatly like a teacher, but you forgot a finger space!" The class responded so well to this strategy that it became a weekly occurrence in our classroom. I had to set up a rotating schedule so they could share their writing and have a turn on the board. This motivated students that were not always engaged in Writing Workshop because they now had a new sense of purpose and excitement. It also became a fantastic way to share and learn about each other. As our writing units progressed, we continued this strategy throughout the school year.

—*Kate Sullivan*

Chapter 4

Supporting a Positive, Productive Climate

In this chapter you will find strategies for supporting a positive, productive classroom climate. These teacher-guided strategies include:

- **Building Positive Teacher-Student Relationships and Trust** (Strategy 16) so students feel safe and valued and contribute positively to the classroom.

    > The best part about teaching is the students, so if you invest in their well-being, everything else falls into place.
    >
    > —*Jennifer Raser*, chapter contributor

- **Building Positive Peer-to-Peer Relationships and Trust** (Strategy 17) so students feel safe taking risks, breaking out of their comfort zone, and working through challenges.

    > When you have a community that knows each other well and more deeply, there is a human connection that will make it feel safer for you, and you make it safer for others. Kids can then relax and learn.
    >
    > —*Lorin Wilson*, chapter contributor

- **Guiding Students to Share Their Thinking and Feelings** (Strategy 18) to deepen their metacognitive thinking, personal reflection, and engagement with one another.

    > I use a ton of anchor charts with visuals. My classroom isn't just about students making their thinking visual, teachers have to model also.
    >
    > —*Emma First*, chapter contributor

- Learning where others are coming from and deepening knowledge and understanding during discussions of **Connecting through Current Events** (Strategy 19).

By giving students a small bite [of current events], it encourages them to go out and find more. If I don't include the current events in my class on any given day, students complain.

—*Adam Klempa*, chapter contributor

- **Supporting Student-Led Learning** (Strategy 20) where students explore ideas on their own while the teacher guides them through the learning and creation of a product that shows mastery.

    My job is to make sure your child has enough resources or knows where to go so they are not waiting around for me . . . it's not going to come easy, but they are going to have to step up and ask the questions they need answered and know where to go to find answers.

    —*Revathi Balakrishnan*, chapter contributor

HIGHLIGHTS

- Learn about how to give students a fresh start after they make a mistake in **Building Positive Teacher-Student Relationships and Trust** (Strategy 16).
- Explore ways to use role play to help students navigate challenging situations in **Building Positive Peer-to-Peer Relationships and Trust** (Strategy 17).
- See how students can learn to share different ways of thinking by talking to the hand [Puppet] in **Guiding Students to Share Their Thinking and Feelings** (Strategy 18).
- Get tips for supporting students as they navigate taking in and sharing multiple perspectives in **Connecting through Current Events** (Strategy 19).
- Consider ways to build community and ensure students are inclusive when they work in groups in **Supporting Student-Led Learning** (Strategy 20).

GUIDING QUESTIONS

As you read through this section, consider the following:

1. What do you bring to the classroom, and how does your personality and experience influence the ways that you interact with your students?
2. In what ways do I support positive peer-to-peer relationships and trust as the year progresses?
3. How do I guide my students in their metacognitive and reflective thinking?
4. How do I support students' intake of information and response to ideas that are different from their own?
5. How do I create an environment in which students look to each other and to themselves for help before looking to me?

STRATEGY 16: BUILDING POSITIVE TEACHER-STUDENT RELATIONSHIPS AND TRUST

> Teacher Contributors
> Bob Feurer, North Bend Central Middle School/High School (NE), 7th, 11th–12th grades
> Jennifer Raser, Wheatland High School (WY), 9th–12th grade

Positive teacher-student relationships are built on trust, consistency, honesty, and grace. When students feel safe and valued in the classroom, they are more likely to contribute constructively to the classroom community and put forth academic effort. The steps that follow are about maintaining positive teacher-student relationships and trust. This strategy builds on what was shared in *Strategy 7: Getting to Know Students*.

Strategy Implementation

Relationships and trust are the result of what you, as the teacher, bring to the classroom and how you interact with your students. Be mindful each day of how you are sharing, connecting, reacting, and responding to others.

Part I: What You Bring to the Classroom

Each day, you set the climate for your classroom. When you bring your best, most genuine self, you invite students to do the same. When you show care in big and small ways, you are letting students know that they are safe with you.

> My students know I love them more than I hate the paperwork.
>
> —Jennifer Raser

1. **Be yourself.** Students can tell when you are genuine. Bring your personality into the classroom. Share your interests; admit your faults; let them know what excites you about this job; and be honest about the parts that don't excite you and how you manage that.

2. **Get to their hearts through their stomachs.** If your budget and school rules allow, keep food in your classroom. A bag of pretzels or a cup of noodles may help meet a need for a student whether that need is staving off hunger or just the feeling of comfort that comes from chatting and sharing a snack. You'd be surprised to see how much magic a package of goldfish crackers holds when it comes to teacher-student relationships!

3. **Connecting through humor.** Laughter unites us! Find the funny in your day! Look for cartoons, memes, and videos that connect with the content and skills students are learning. Laugh at yourself when you struggle. Of course, it is important to know your audience. Teachers are some of the

> When a joke is bad, it's still good because I can admit it was pretty lame and we can laugh at that together.
>
> —Bob Feurer

worst culprits of sarcasm in the classroom, and sarcasm can be extremely hurtful if misunderstood or directed at a person who does not find sarcasm funny. Make students aware of your comedic style and ensure they are comfortable with it.

4. **Make time outside of class.** It's easy to find out if someone has a soccer game, is playing chess, or has a birthday party coming up. Make time to see your students engaging in extracurricular activities, and to talk with them about what excites them. (See *Strategy 7: Getting to Know Students* for more information on how to connect with students through extracurricular activities.)

Part II: How You and Your Students Interact

Though you may be a strong force in setting the tone for your class, ultimately, the climate is determined by the ways you and your students collaborate. Intentional commitment to positive interactions will create an environment that is safe and comfortable for all.

1. **Create a culture of honesty and vulnerability.** Let students see you struggle, and show them how you adapt.
   - *Feelings:* Be honest about how you feel and show what you do with those feelings (e.g., pause to take a deep breath if you are frustrated, or step away and work on something else for a minute).
   - *Difficulties:* Share things that are difficult for you (e.g., struggle with a math problem; work through pronouncing a new word; or draw something badly).
   - *Getting Stuck:* Model what you do when you get stuck or how to make something better (e.g., break down the problem or word into parts or use a picture as a model for your drawing).

2. **Give grace and allow for a fresh start every day.** Everyone messes up! If you or a student have a bad day, find a way to face your actions and then leave those actions in the past.
   - *Express Disappointment in the Action:* Let students know when you are disappointed with their action or their choice. Express displeasure with *what they did* and not in *who they are*.
   - *Maintain Consistent Expectations and Consequences:* If there is a consequence for the student's action, let the student know that they will have to face the consequence. Stay consistent with applying the consequences while allowing for flexibility based on individual students' needs.
   - *Move On:* Once you and your student have addressed a poor choice or action, move on. This can be easier said than done, but it is extremely important for maintaining positive relationships. Sometimes it helps to remember that if a student has a tough day in your

> Always remember, this is somebody's kid. You have a responsibility to not only teach them but to care for them. You have to hold them responsible, but you also have to give them a fresh start every day.
>
> —Jennifer Raser

classroom, that might mean that student feels safe enough in that space to have a tough day there.

Considering Different Types of Learners

Though each of the adaptations are likely to benefit all students, the "X" marks indicate adaptations to this strategy that are particularly helpful for English-language learners, Special Education students, and Gifted and Talented students.

English-Language Learners				
Provide visuals	Label materials in multiple languages	Translate instructions/ materials to their primary language	Model expectations/ processes	Invite students to write/speak in primary language
			X	X
Special Education Students				
Scaffold instructions/ chunking	Provide positive reinforcement	Schedule breaks	Offer multiple options/formats for student to choose	Minimize distractions
	X		X	
Gifted and Talented Students				
Encourage students to focus on learning rather than grades	Celebrate nonacademic successes with students	Provide opportunities for students to take individualized ownership of learning	Challenge students to use more sophisticated vocabulary	Invite students to share how their thinking is extended by hearing new perspectives
	X			X

STRATEGY IN ACTION: "DON'T MAKE ME WALK BACK THERE!"

Some of the most powerful words I've used in my classroom are "Don't make me walk back there!" This simple phrase redirects students through humor. My science classroom had six lab tables with four students at each table. I *wanted* the environment to be active, engaged, and fun; I *needed* the environment to be safe and focused. Saying "Don't make me walk back there!" in a tone that was both stern and humorous worked in just about any situation when a student or students were off task or misbehaving. There is a bit of a veiled threat in the comment. It gets students' attention, calls their behavior into question, and inherently works to have them self-evaluate what they are or aren't doing.

—*Bob Feurer*

How to Implement the Strategy at Varied Grade Levels

Elementary	Middle	High
*Incorporate students' names and interests on worksheets. Show them that you know who they are and that you care enough to include it! *Create a signal that reminds students that they have a fresh start once they've faced a consequence. For example, you could be a mime wiping a board clean.	*Consistently focus on how to cope with frustration and recover from mistakes. Middle school is a time when students are extremely self-conscious about being judged by others. Show them how you handle this. *With humor, know your audience! Be sure you are sensitive to your students' personalities.	*Provide opportunities for students to share how they engage in productive struggle. (See *Strategy 4: Failing Forward* on pages 14–15) *Discuss resiliency and healthy relationships and how to support these in students' lives.

WHY I LIKE THIS STRATEGY

When students know that you genuinely care about them, they are free to learn. It doesn't cost anything to develop relationships and you don't have to add anything to your curriculum. The best part about teaching is the students, so if you invest in their well-being, everything else falls into place.

—*Jennifer Raser*

I use humor to connect with my students because humor is one of the *16 Habits of Mind* (Costal & Kalick, 2008) that all intelligent people demonstrate. Humor reduces stress and can be quite educational if used correctly. It's interdisciplinary, not age-dependent, and is where you find it.

—*Bob Feurer*

Adaptation for Different Assets and Needs

Student Personality	
Reserved	*Open*
*Create opportunities for private sharing through a teacher-student journal. Write back and forth to each other. *Do individual check-ins with students outside of class, in the hallways, as they enter class, and during independent work.	*Enjoy these connections. Help students who might be more talkative to make space for quieter students and encourage those peers to share. *Be cognizant of where to draw the line in terms of what you both share.

Time	
Limited Time	*Lots of Time*
*Remember that time spent building relationships is time well spent. When you know about your students, you can better connect their learning to their interests and the instructional time is higher quality because of the time you spend relating with your students. *Be intentional about how you allocate time so you are able to include relationship-building opportunities into your lessons.	*Dedicate the time you have to engaging in real conversations with students about what matters to them. *Discuss and debrief the ways that lessons connect with students' lives.

STRATEGY IN ACTION: A FRESH START

I had a student that, in the past, had very violent and explosive episodes. He would get frustrated with any assignment that couldn't be done fast because he struggled to focus. By the time I had him in my class each day, he was very fatigued. Over the years, I got to know him and what his interests were. We were able to joke and work through assignments and he would experience some frustration, but nothing overwhelming. One day, he became agitated with an assignment and was extremely rude to me. I avoided engaging in confrontation by getting up from the table and going to help another student. The bell rang; the class left; the remainder of the day was uneventful.

The next day, when this student came to class, he looked at me and apologized for being disrespectful to me. He said he was really frustrated with his assignment and he took it out on me. I looked at him and told him that I accepted his apology, that I knew it wasn't easy for him to apologize, and that I appreciated it.

My big take-away from this was that because we had built a relationship over the years, he felt safe enough to let his frustrations out, and he cared enough to apologize for it. Did he care because I cared? I'd like to think so. All students, Special Education or not, need grace and a fresh start every day.

—*Jennifer Raser*

STRATEGY 17: BUILDING PEER-TO-PEER RELATIONSHIPS AND TRUST

> Teacher Contributors
> *Kristen Frade, Mary McDowell Friends School (NY), Kindergarten–1st grades*
> *Lorin Wilson, Parkside Intermediate School (CA), 6th–8th grades*

A critical element of a positive classroom climate is students building strong relationships and trust with one another. Building relationships and trust starts at the beginning of the year and must be reinforced and grow over the course of the year. Typically, the first step is having students develop their peer relationships and those relationships grow into trust.

Strategy Implementation

As the teacher, you have an incredible opportunity to foster relationships among students that deepen their connection and trust. This results in an environment where students feel safe taking risks, breaking out of their comfort zone, and working through challenges.

Part I: Setting the Tone

Each year, you have a new group of students who are anxious and excited to start the year with one another. Some know each other, and some do not. Prioritizing relationship building from day one sets a positive, collaborative tone for the year.

1. **Start the year with relationship building.** Rather than jumping into the content at the beginning of the school year, start by focusing on building community and giving students a chance to get to know one another. (See *Strategy 3: Getting to Know Students* and *Strategy 8: Team Building Games* for more ideas of how to do this.)

2. **Prioritize teacher-student relationships.** For students to trust what you do in the classroom, you must first focus on developing your own relationships with students (see *Strategy 16: Building Positive Teacher-Student Relationships* with ways to do this). Students must know that you love them and want what's best for them; at that point, they will be willing to buy into what you plan to do in your class, including getting to know one another.

3. **Don't rush relationship building.** As Lorin Wilson said, "It's about *building* community and not *forcing* kids into community." And to do this, you must take the time to do it right. Start with getting to know the superficial things about one another (see *Strategy 7: Getting to Know Students*). Once students have built that comfort with one another, create spaces and activities that give them opportunities to open up more and dig deeper into each other's cultural backgrounds and interests (e.g., sharing oral histories they have conducted about their family).

4. **Pushing students out of their comfort zone.** To have a successful life you need to learn how to tolerate some discomfort. This allows us to learn something new, manage being uncomfortable, and be resilient and pushed to try new things. Once students have started to build relationships with one another, create groupings and exercises that challenge them to work things out and find solutions, even if it isn't easy.

5. **Learning about one another while connecting to the content.** Another great way for students to build deeper relationships with each other is by connecting your class content with students' lives, giving students a chance to share more about their backgrounds. This will help deepen relationships and trust between students. (See *Strategy 11: Student Voice to Start Class* for ideas related to this.)

6. **Developing trust.** Trust is something that takes time to build and typically comes after individuals have developed a relationship. As the year progresses, begin to integrate activities that require students to rely on one another and take risks, academically and emotionally, to build that trust together. These might include:
    - Share stories of failure, what you learned, and what you did to move forward (See *Strategy 4: Failing Forward*).
    - Use Kalina Silverman's *Big Talk* for ideas about engaging in meaningful conversations that require trust: https://www.makebigtalk.com/.

> When they become adults they need to learn how to get along and work with one another (whether you like them or not). Therefore, it's important to provide students with guided opportunities to help them build relationships with others.
>
> —Lorin Wilson

Part II: Meeting New People with Creative Groupings

In the classroom, students often stay with the people they know unless they are strategically placed in groups and activities with new people. Therefore, it is important to thoughtfully create spaces for all students to get to know each other, collaborate, and build trust. An example of how you might do this follows.

1. **Strategies for putting students in groups to meet and work with new people.** There are many ways you can creatively put students into groups so they can work on developing relationships with one another. One example is:
    - *Playing Card Table Topper:* This approach helps put students into strategic (and sometimes random) groups, base table groups, or mixing up groups for shorter activities on a daily basis. This is how it works:
        ○ Get two decks of playing cards.
        ○ Plan your specialized groupings:
            - Decide whether you want students grouped together who share similarities or if you want to intentionally put students together who are different in many ways. Come up with groups of four (ideally).

- Assign cards to students within groups. Have all different numbers and suits, and two red and two black in each table group of four. (If you have table groups of three, give all different numbers, different suits, and two of one color and one of the other color).
  ➢ NOTE: Only use numbered cards, so you can have students use math to combine cards and get into groups.
- Tape cards down:
  - Layout the cards on each desk or table.
  - Review your primary seating or group arrangements.
  - Using packing tape, secure each card to the table where students can easily see it.
- With the second deck of cards, give each student their assigned card, and ask them to find their desk with the matching card. This will be their base group seat. Students will hold onto the assigned card for when they switch up groupings. You may want them to tape their card to a class notebook or laptop.
- Practice the procedure in class:
  - Give students their card (suit and number) and have them practice finding their seat with the matching card (base groups).
  - Let students know they will be mixing up their groups for different activities on a daily basis based on their cards. Practice getting into and out of various groupings. You can say:
    ➢ "All those with the same number find your group. Spades will stay in their seats, all the others with the same number will join them."
    ➢ "Black cards to the front of the class. Red to the back."
    ➢ "Diamonds bring your reading book to the back. Everyone else do the questions on pages 12 and 13."
  - Assign small getting to know you tasks for every grouping they get into.

2. **Working through challenging groupings.** A big part of building strong relationships and trust is working through challenges together. Some ways to do this include:
   - *Individual Problem between Students:* If there are problems between two students, don't just switch their groups or separate the students (though that might be necessary initially depending on the conflict). Ask the students to express what the conflict is, share their thoughts on why and how it is affecting them, and then have them come up with solutions for how they can move forward together. During these discussions, work on students developing skills for reframing their language in a positive and inclusive way and get students to "walk in each other's shoes" to understand the impact of some of their language choices.
   - *Consistent Problem across Groups:* If you are noticing similar challenges or conflicts across multiple groups, you can use role plays to help students learn how to work through conflict so everyone gets a win.

> *Consensus* is not when everyone agrees; it is coming to an idea everyone can live with—you need to have everyone move in the same direction.
>
> —*Lorin Wilson*

- NOTE: If doing a whole class role play or discussion about problematic behaviors, don't use the offending student's name, rather, talk in generalities. You may also want to wait until some time has passed, so the connection to positive next steps is made, without calling out the students who need redirection.

> Part of teaching is equipping kids with strategies for when there's disagreement or conflict.
>
> —Lorin Wilson

STRATEGY IN ACTION: PLAYING CARD TABLE TOPPERS

As with most good/great teaching strategies, I picked this up from another teacher! I have used this in both the 5th-grade self-contained classroom as well as 6th-grade subject-based classrooms. Initially, I used this strategy for those getting to know you activities at the beginning of the year.

I start by asking them, "Working with your table group, what's the largest number you can create with the numbers supplied? All of you raise your hands when you agree. When I call on your table group, tell me what that number is." The first day of 6th grade, most students are a little intimidated by middle school, so I keep things light and easy by asking simple questions like "What number do you have if you reverse those digits?" or, "What's the sum/product of all of your numbers?"

Then, when I want them to begin to learn fun facts about each other, I might call out, "Get together with all the numbers identical to your assigned number and find out the birthday of who is the oldest in this new group."

I try to keep the first few days' questions fairly innocuous such as favorite ice cream, pizza, fast food, etc. If I get a response of, "I don't feel comfortable sharing that information" (perhaps on, "Did you do anything fun this summer?" and maybe a student was having to deal with a death in the family, or a foster child was changing homes), I'll ask them if they can share it quietly with me, then, if appropriate, share with just their group. If that still doesn't work, I'll be sure to ask an "easier" question for the next round or two, to get them involved again.

In most class sorting activities, there are always a few who want to make it known, they are not going to participate. For example, they won't move from where they are. That's OK, because everyone else can move to them! Depending on the overall tone of class, I decide how many rounds to do this activity and what types of questions to ask.

—Lorin Wilson

Part III: Developing Relationship and Trust Skills through Role Playing

Role playing provides a way for everyone in the classroom to see and practice how to react in social situations, which directly help with building stronger relationships and trust among students.

1. **Brainstorm social scenarios.** It is important to determine meaningful scenarios that help students develop relationship skills. To do this:

- *Look at Trends:* Think about your students, the age group, and areas where you consistently notice students struggling with relationship dynamics (e.g., sharing, not knowing the language necessary to initiate peer play, expanding language skills to help peers relate to their classmates, working through disagreements, how to build conversations, etc.)
- *Consider Recent or Anticipated Struggles:* Target situations you have observed the group struggling with earlier in the week or situations you expect may arise due to an upcoming change in the schedule or future event.
- *Let Students Choose:* Often, students know best. They might not know how to articulate what they need help with, but they can identify a situation that frustrated them. Give students opportunities to identify these scenarios to use as role plays.

Why Use Role Playing

We tried targeting the language, flexibility, and empathy necessary to resolve social situations in other ways using props such as puppets, and by viewing related videos, reading picture books, etc. These methods can be effective, but once we started acting the situations out ourselves, and asking the students to provide solutions, their engagement increased and we observed them referencing and reflecting on the lessons more often. Using this strategy enables us to explicitly target social situations occurring in our classroom, so we can provide better support to our students. This strategy also helps us preview prosocial behaviors, language, and coping skills to help our students understand the expectations for responding to events.

—*Kristen Frade*

How Often to Do Role Plays

- Schedule them once or twice a week, if possible.
- Be open to doing role plays in the moment when a situation arises.
- Move toward students taking more ownership of creating and leading role plays.

---

2. **Role play a challenging situation.** To help students think about and consider the right way to engage in a social scenario, it is useful to invite them to think about what makes the situation challenging:
   - *Introduce the Social Scenario:* Use a slide deck, read a story, or watch a video to introduce the social problem you will be role playing. Ask students, "What do you think we should do?" Encourage them to keep their ideas in mind as the initial role play takes place.
     - NOTE: Connect the chosen behavior to your classroom agreements so they can see the importance of focusing on them to retain positive peer relationships and trust.

- *Set the Tone:* As the teacher, let students know you have struggled with this too, being vulnerable in front of your students and honest with them is a way to forge trust over time.
- *Act Out the Scenario:* Consider acting out the scenario with a co-teacher, paraprofessional, or student who volunteers to help you demonstrate the *wrong* way to react to the situation. Instruct the audience to pay attention to what they: notice, think went wrong, and would do differently.

> Watching people make mistakes, knowing teachers are willing to do that, goes a long way with the trusting classroom community where it's OK to make mistakes, and kids need to be told that!
>
> —Kristen Frade

3. **Debrief the role play.** End the scene and have a conversation with the students about what they saw, noticed, and felt about the scenario. During the debrief, focus on:
    - What students are thinking about the situation, as their takeaways may be quite different from the adults in the room, and from each other.
    - How others might be feeling and thinking differently about the same situation.
    - Giving students more vocabulary about their emotions and strategies to shift from one emotion to the other.
    - Connecting to previous discussions that align with the current one.

4. **Students Engage in a Redo.** Ask the students to do a redo where they react in a different way to resolve the problem. Redos could be students with a teacher or students with each other.
    - *Selecting Student Volunteers:* Ask students (typically two) if they want to volunteer to act out the redo. If you only get one volunteer, you can do the redo with the volunteer.
        - Choose based on who raises their hand. Students might be shy and not want to do it or not have ideas.
        - For students who are less engaged, try to build their comfort with the role play by making it fun and meaningful. As they get used to it, they will get more excited about it.
    - *Preparation for Redo*: Give the students who volunteer to do the redo a minute or two to prepare their role play. While the actors are doing this, ask the rest of the class to discuss in pairs or small groups what they think might happen.
    - *Act Out the Redo Scenario:* Have the student volunteers act out their new role play. Again, instruct the audience to pay attention to what they: notice, think went wrong, and would do differently.

5. **Debrief redo.** After the redo, discuss students' reactions to it, how it impacted them, and then how they can transfer the skill to other situations or settings. In the debrief, focus on:
    - What was done differently from the initial role play and why it worked better.
    - If the redo did *not* work, *why* didn't it work and what might need to be done differently.

6. **Repeat redos (as needed).** Based on how well the class thinks a redo resolves the scenario, you may need to engage in a second or third redo. The number of redos will be based on the need as well as the time you have. (If you don't have time, you can pause and return to the same scenario later in the week.)

7. **Highlight and practice the language and skills to work on.** Before transitioning into your next class activity, focus on concrete language and skills for students to work on and practice. This helps students understand that the skills you are discussing and developing are a work in progress and something to keep developing throughout the year, and outside the classroom.
   - *Tease Out Language and Skills:* Explicitly tease out language that will help students better navigate the scenario in the future and enhance their relationships with one another. For instance, if your scenario was about helping students more effectively talk about their feelings, you can tell students how to use "I feel . . ." statements, and then reinforce how to use them in different situations.
   - *Practice:* Let students know there will be spaces to practice these skills in class, and to work on them outside of class. The goal is that students practice the new skills and language so much it becomes routine. With that, peer relationships are strengthened and trust is enhanced.

8. **Acknowledge and reinforce during class (after role playing).** For students to apply their new relationship skills and build that trust with one another, it is important to acknowledge and reinforce when students positively use language and skills and to support them when they are struggling. Some ways to do this include:
   - Point out when you notice students positively using the skills and language from the role plays and give positive affirmations for it; students can point it out to their peers as well.
     - You can say, "I love how you communicated with your friend."
     - Share with parents explicit examples of how their kids are being successful in these areas. (According to Kristen Frade, parents of her students tell her that their children bring their new skills and language home and use and practice them in their home life.)

It's OK to Make Mistakes

Role playing makes students feel comfortable to take risks and do things differently, breaking patterns they are in. Their comfort level increases and they just know it's OK to make mistakes; they can try to do things differently. It's not about turning it into a negative thing; let students know, "it's hard for everybody." The biggest part of the job is that everyone is going to make mistakes and that's a normal thing that will happen your whole life when you're relating to people. Persevere and do things differently; figure out what you can do to fix it. With this in mind, we use the term "redo" a lot.

—*Kristen Frade*

- If you or students notice students struggling with applying the new skill or language from a scenario you role played in class, students (or you) can say, "Let's practice it together." Then build in time to work on practicing that skill and/or language, even if it requires pausing the curriculum.

STRATEGY IN ACTION: ACTING OUT SOCIAL EMOTIONAL LEARNING SCENARIOS

We were teaching our Social Emotional Learning class and targeting expanding pragmatic language skills. Some of our students were struggling with maintaining eye contact, not responding to peers' questions, and answering with one-word answers. We couldn't find many picture books that targeted these language skills so we decided to act out the scenario ourselves.

The class was *riveted* and fully engaged. Many students raised their hands when we asked them to share about what they noticed and described how we were feeling accurately. A student asked to join us "on the stage" (which was just our meeting area rug) and they offered to act out a redo. Soon almost every student was asking to come up and do a redo. They couldn't get enough of it and we extended the period for quite a while, so everyone could get a turn.

We've now been using the strategy for many years, around a variety of different topics. The students love seeing their teachers purposefully making mistakes, doing the wrong thing, being dramatic. At times the students' redos don't work, and don't resolve the situation. We go with this and brainstorm more ideas, use it as an opportunity rather than shutting down their initial idea. I think this helps the students understand it's okay to make mistakes or to be unsure of how to handle or talk about a situation. Letting them experiment and work through it with the support of their teachers and classmates helps to build a safe and trusting classroom community.

—Kristen Frade

How to Implement the Strategy at Varied Grade Levels

Elementary	Middle	High
*Include relationship building into your daily or weekly schedule. *Build activities and experiences into your curriculum that give opportunities for students to practice relationship and trust skills.	*Let students start to take more ownership of the process, pointing out and practicing skills needed to work on to develop relationships and trust. *Make time for debriefs about relationship building to be more student-driven.	*Focus on the importance of relationships and trust building in relation to student success as adults and in life outside the classroom. *Connect the relationship building more to the class content and application to students' lived experiences.

Considering Different Types of Learners

Though each of the adaptations are likely to benefit all students, the "X" marks indicate adaptations to this strategy that are particularly helpful for English-language learners, Special Education students, and Gifted and Talented students.

English-Language Learners				
Provide visuals	Label materials in multiple languages	Translate instructions/ materials to their primary language	Model expectations/ processes	Invite students to write/speak in primary language
		X	X	X
Special Education Students				
Scaffold instructions/ chunking	Provide positive reinforcement	Schedule breaks	Offer multiple options/formats for student to choose	Minimize distractions
X	X		X	X
Gifted and Talented Students				
Encourage students to focus on learning rather than grades	Celebrate nonacademic successes with students	Provide opportunities for students to take individualized ownership of learning	Challenge students to use more sophisticated vocabulary	Invite students to share how their thinking is extended by hearing new perspectives
X	X			X

WHY I LIKE THIS STRATEGY

In middle school, things are really awkward, and if you don't take time to build community, students don't feel safe and secure. They then begin to worry more about others' thoughts about them than learning and trying their best. When you have a community that knows each other well and more deeply, there is a human connection that will make it feel safer for you, and you make it safer for others. Kids can then relax and learn. Plus, nobody has all the answers, so you have to have a community feeling where students can be authentic, present, and take risks, and ask questions with one another and the teacher.

—*Lorin Wilson*

Using role playing to work on peer-to-peer relationships is great because students build the trust to try and develop these skills. It's so successful because they are the ones acting it out eventually. Audience members are not just passively watching; they're thinking about their relationships with their classmates. They need that spiraling curriculum where they touch on the relationships, language skills, and empathy over and over again, actively using the words, doing things with their bodies, and recognizing what others are doing, or what their face looks like. They need lots of practice with it and spaces to use their bodies, using sensory skills, and getting muscle memory where you practice and your body just knows how to react to the situations—it's a whole body experience.

—*Kristen Frade*

Adaptation for Different Assets and Needs

Size of Class	
Small Class	**Large Class**
*Let students spend significant time with each other in small settings (pairs or small groups).	*Mix up groups a lot, enabling students to interact with everyone in class (if possible) at least once a week.
*Give students more space to point out and highlight relationship challenges they are experiencing and then take ownership of developing skills to navigate the situation.	*Keep groups small.

Cultural Diversity	
Limited Diversity	**Lots of Diversity**
*Focus on how students are diverse in different ways.	*Talk about how you are part of a larger world and how students have different practices at home, eat different foods, etc.
*Introduce new cultures and experiences they might encounter in the future, and how students can be inclusive.	*Address differences in a sensitive way.

STRATEGY 18: GUIDING STUDENTS TO SHARE THEIR THINKING AND FEELINGS

> Teacher Contributors
> *Daniel Leija, Carson Elementary Northside ISD (TX),
> Kindergarten–5th grades*
> *Emma First, Delran Hight School (NJ) 9th–12th grades*

People think and act in different ways. Giving students opportunities to share their thinking and feelings and ask each other questions provides a basis for understanding and offers options for next steps. When students have strong models and frames for how to talk about their thoughts and feelings, they deepen their metacognitive thinking, personal reflection, and engagement with one another.

Strategy Implementation

1. **Let students know the value of being able to articulate thoughts and feelings.** Many people process information by saying it out loud. When you share what you are thinking or label what you are feeling, it can clarify your own understanding. Help students understand this through examples like:
   - Deconstructing the experience of reading aloud (e.g., When you read the dialogue of a book aloud, you likely do so with more emphasis on the meaning and emotion behind the words as compared with when you read the book in your head. Speaking the words aloud can help strengthen comprehension.).
   - Sharing a clip from a movie that shows a character having an "aha moment" while speaking aloud (e.g., In the movie *Inside Out*, there is a great "aha moment" when Joy, the main character, is describing what she is thinking and she realizes that all feelings are needed to have balance.).

2. **Emphasize the process.** Often what is most important in learning and developing isn't finding the right answer, it's learning from the process. Share stories of how the process yielded important results and how being able to describe thoughts and feelings led to success.
   - *Read* The Empty Pot *Together:* In this story, an emperor declares his successor will be the person who grows the best flower from seeds that he gives to the citizens. After a year, people share their plants, and a child comes with an empty pot. He explains that he planted the seed and cared for it, but it did not grow. The child is chosen to be the emperor because of his honesty.
   - *Watch a* TED Talk*:* Most *TED Talks* are not about the end result of someone's work, they are about the journey and the process that led to a particular result. Share a *TED Talk* about a topic of interest to your students and discuss how the speaker made their thinking and feelings clear for the listener.
   - *Model Talking through Your Own Thinking and Feelings:* Never underestimate how much your students want to learn about you. Share stories of how you came to understand something or how you felt in a particular situation. This sharing will help you connect with your students, help them to feel safe in sharing with

you and others, and give them language and frames for sharing their own thinking and feelings.
- *Model Thinking:* Make clear what you were trying to understand, how you used what you already knew, questions you asked yourself, or strategies you employed to improve your understanding. For example:
  - Rather than just telling students the formula for the area for a triangle, tell them that you know the formula for the area of a rectangle is base × height. Then model with tiles how two equal triangles together form a rectangle, so the formula for finding the area of a triangle is just cutting that in half.
- *Model Feelings:* Tell stories of how you responded to a situation in a way that makes you proud or that you now regret. Unpack the emotions you felt and how they influenced your words and actions. Use a feelings chart or word bank to help with this. Be explicit in sharing how feelings escalated and diminished for you. This will help students develop more precise language. For example:
  ◦ On the first day of school, you feel nervous, scared, excited, hopeful, and many more emotions. Talk about which of these increase as the first week goes on and which diminish. Start with something that is fairly low stakes and lead to more complex discussions of feelings related to various situations in school and outside of school.

> I tell my kids the story of a teacher telling me I was dumb. This lit the fire! I was going to prove him wrong.
>
> —Daniel Leija

3. **Give opportunities for students to share.** Whether discussing their thought processes or feelings, create opportunities for students to share with each other in varied ways. The following advice will lead to successful sharing in each format:
   - *Small Group Sharing:* Limit groups to three people, so students have the time to share in detail and respond to one another.
   - *Presenting to the Whole Class:* Be sure that students are prepared to share and that they feel comfortable before you call on them.
   - *Creating Posters to Represent Thinking and Feelings:* Share models of posters, and deconstruct the elements that help to make thinking and feelings clear. Emphasize the importance of these essential elements more than the format or look of the poster.
   - *Sharing Online via Shared Written Documents, Photos with Captions, or Video:* As with posters, be sure to emphasize the key elements that will clearly articulate thinking and reflections on feelings.
     ◦ NOTE: Set guidelines for how electronic documents are shared, so student information does not become more public than intended.
4. **Encourage clarification and discussion.** The purpose of encouraging students to share their thinking and feelings is to help them learn more about themselves and others. This can be supported by developing a set of questions to ask in order to deepen understanding of thinking or feelings. Consider the following:
   - "Why did you do it this way?"
   - "How did you come up with . . . ?"

- "What if you tried . . . ?"
- "I'm thinking . . . How does this connect?"

When students lead the discussion through targeted questioning, the teacher becomes a coach or guide who facilitates the sharing and reflection as needed.

> Every class is its own little ecosystem.
>
> —*Emma First*

5. **Use what you learn.** Using a great idea that a classmate or colleague shares isn't stealing; it's acting on inspiration. Encourage students to adapt and use the approaches that their peers share with them. These approaches may relate to learning content, skills development, or managing emotions. Encourage students to tell each other when they use a peer's idea or approach. This will give greater value to and lead to even more supportive sharing.

6. **Keep track of what works.** If several students agree on an approach that they like for solving an equation, starting an essay, or responding mindfully to an emotionally challenging situation, find a place to post that approach in the room. You might have a bulletin board dedicated to "Life and Learning Hacks." Ask students to write out the steps to the approach and have peers post examples of how they've used it.

> I use a ton of anchor charts with visuals. My classroom isn't just about *students* making their thinking visual, *teachers* have to model also.
>
> —*Emma First*

STRATEGY IN ACTION: COLLABORATING ISN'T CHEATING

In our classroom, students are often seated in pairs. They would whisper to each other while working, asking about the meaning of particular words or phrases, or confirming their understanding. I think students were concerned that this would seem like cheating, so they tried to do it covertly. Eventually, we had a class discussion, and I shared that I was proud of them for supporting each other. They had created a working system of figuring out the most important parts of a text by whittling it down together, and then coming up with their own, individual ideas and ways of showing their understanding.

—*Emma First*

Considering Different Types of Learners

Though each of the adaptations are likely to benefit all students, the "X" marks indicate adaptations to this strategy that are particularly helpful for English-language learners, Special Education students, and Gifted and Talented students.

English-Language Learners				
Provide visuals	Label materials in multiple languages	Translate instructions/ materials to their primary language	Model expectations/ processes	Invite students to write/speak in primary language
X		X	X	X
Special Education Students				
Scaffold instructions/ chunking	Provide positive reinforcement	Schedule breaks	Offer multiple options/formats for student to choose	Minimize distractions
X	X	X	X	X
Gifted and Talented Students				
Encourage students to focus on learning rather than grades	Celebrate nonacademic successes with students	Provide opportunities for students to take individualized ownership of learning	Challenge students to use more sophisticated vocabulary	Invite students to share how their thinking is extended by hearing new perspectives
X	X		X	X

How to Implement the Strategy at Varied Grade Levels

Elementary	Middle	High
*Use sentence starters to guide students in sharing their thinking or feelings. *Give opportunities for students to draw or talk through their thinking or feelings rather than writing.	*Remember, this type of attention, especially when focused on feelings, can be overwhelming for middle schoolers. Give students the opportunity to present their thinking or feelings in pairs or small groups before presenting to the whole class. *Work together to develop a word bank of detailed and specific language that describes feelings.	*Discuss the benefits of metacognitive thinking and how students can improve their approaches to challenges by reflecting on their own processes and learning from one another. *Incorporate more sophisticated vocabulary to describe feelings accurately.

> ## WHY I LIKE THIS STRATEGY
>
> We don't all think the same way. There's always more than one way to get to the answer. I tell my students, I'll show you a few ways, and if you can show me a way that works for you, we'll go with it. Once students begin to make sense of their thinking, they become less anxious about the subject/topic.
>
> —*Daniel Leija*
>
> My biggest takeaway from encouraging students to share their thinking is how it decreases the pressure students feel. When the pressure is off, that wall comes down, and they are accomplishing the same task, but in a more user-friendly way.
>
> —*Emma First*

Adaptation for Different Assets and Needs

Technology

Low-Tech
- Students can create posters of their thinking or feelings and then use sticky notes to comment on one another's approaches.
- Students can search through magazines for images that relate to their thinking or feelings and create a hardcopy of a meme that connects.

High-Tech
- Students can share their thinking or feelings via shared platforms like Flipgrid, Google Docs, etc., and comment on similarities and differences they see in each other's approaches.
- Students can use Bitmojis or memes to represent their thinking or feelings.

Time

Limited Time
- Have students jot down their thinking or feelings on an exit ticket. Review and share commonalities and differences with the class.
- Do five-minute *quick shares*. Pause what students are doing and ask them to turn and talk with a peer about their thinking or feelings for two minutes. Then ask students to share important takeaways from their paired conversations with the whole class for three minutes. This can have a substantial impact in a total of just five minutes.

Lots of Time
- Give opportunities for students to practice and share their thinking or feelings in small groups and then present to the whole class connections and new ideas they learned by working in their small groups. This encourages critical thinking on top of their own personal reflection.
- Set aside time for students to share ideas or practices they *learned* from one another based on their sharing and what happened when they used them.

STRATEGY IN ACTION: TALK TO THE HAND [PUPPET]

If there's anything that is going to get a kid to talk to you, it's a puppet! I have a puppet named Bobby that looks like a little monkey. I introduce Bobby to students on Day 1. "This is Bobby. He comes from a completely different universe. He is here on a mission, and he needs to learn our way of doing math. All year long, I will bring Bobby out and ask you to explain your thinking to him."

To help students share different ways of thinking, I would change things up with Bobby. For example, I might say, "This is Bobby from a different universe. I'm teaching him words. The only word he knows right now is four. You can ask him a question, but the answer has to be four." If students asked a question and the answer wasn't four, Bobby would scratch his head and look at me, but not answer.

—Daniel Leija

STRATEGY 19: CONNECTING THROUGH CURRENT EVENTS

> **Teacher Contributors**
> *Marissa Herrera, Coronado Elementary School (AZ), 3rd grade*
> *Adam Klempa, American School of Paris, (France), 9th–12th grades*

Students are eager to know more about the world around them and that includes understanding and discussing current events. The purpose of discussing current events is to engage in critical dialogue, learn multiple perspectives, and give greater context to the academic learning that takes place in your classroom. Discussions about current events can become divisive when students try to get others to agree with them or to change others' opinions. To engage in meaningful conversations about current events, it is important to ensure that students are comfortable with one another, well-informed, and open to varied perspectives.

Strategy Implementation

1. **Create safe spaces for open conversation.** Before jumping into discussions about current events, it is important for students to agree on how to have respectful conversations.
   - *Group Agreements:* At the start of the year, ensure your class's group agreements include respecting others, giving students equitable time to share, and listening with an open mind (see *Strategy 1: Group Agreements*). These agreements will guide the discussion of current events, so be sure to practice and point out when students are using the agreements in class effectively.
   - *Develop Gradually:* Engage in low-stakes conversations before moving into more complex topics. When having these low-stakes conversations, be explicit about the conversational moves that allow for people to be respectful of others' thoughts and opinions.
   - *Provide Support:* Use discussion starters to get students talking. (e.g., "I think _____ because _____." or "I want to better understand what _____ said.")

> **Everyone Contributes and Everyone Listens**
>
> Set the expectation that every student will participate in the conversation. Ask students to signal when they are ready to contribute (e.g., raise hand, hold up a card). This will particularly benefit and support quieter students with entering the conversation. The facilitator (you or a student with the assigned job) will monitor the signals and have a system for noting who wants to speak and ensuring everyone gets a turn.

- *Inclusive Conversation:* Whenever engaging in low-stakes or more complex conversations, note which students are participating and who might need some encouragement. Invite quieter students into the conversation by:
  - Assigning quick writes or prewrites before the conversation so all students are prepared with something to share.
  - Working the room and paying attention to what students are saying or writing before the conversation.
  - Pointing out ideas that students wrote about individually or shared in small groups that relate to the topic.

2. **Support students in respecting multiple perspectives.** The purpose of discussing current events is not about getting the class to align with one way of thinking. Rather, it is to help students gain understanding of multiple perspectives and learn how to have respectful discussions, even when they do not see eye-to-eye. When students share their opinions, be sure to help them to listen to one another.
   - *Emphasize the Importance of Supporting Opinions with Evidence:* Make clear that students are sharing opinions. Their viewpoint may be different from others, so it is important to be able to share evidence that relates to their viewpoints to help others understand their thinking and rationale.
     - NOTE: Providing evidence does not turn one person's opinion into a "fact." Rather, it helps to clarify the thinking that led to this opinion.
   - *Active Listening:* Discuss with students the body language and verbal responses that show others that they are listening.
     - Body Language
       - Eye contact
       - Nodding
       - Avoid looking at distractions like other students or devices.
     - Verbal Responses
       - "Mmmm Hmmmm"
       - "Tell me more about . . ."
       - "I want to understand what you mean by . . ."
       - "I think I heard you say . . ."
   - *Navigating the Discussion of Multiple Perspectives:* It can be challenging for students who disagree to keep the conversation moving and productive (rather than a combative back and forth). Short conversation moves can help the dialogue remain productive:
     - Start with a positive (e.g., "I like what you said about . . .").
     - Rephrase and question (e.g., "I think I heard you say . . . ; How does that relate to . . . ?").
     - Find common ground (e.g., "We both felt strongly about . . . ; What about . . . ?").
     - Disagree respectfully (e.g., "I think we see things differently when it comes to . . . ; I want to compare how we look at this.").

- *Remind and Redirect:* If students interrupt or contradict a speaker, remind them that they are practicing their listening skills and that they will get a chance to share their ideas later. Praise students who step up to share and students who step back to make room for new speakers.

3. **Use balanced sources.** When you discuss current events, it is important for you and your students to be well informed. Find resources that are educational and represent the facts and policies regarding the event or issue rather than opinion. Media sources have different biases and perspectives, just like you and your students. Examine media sources within your community and determine where they are on the political spectrum. Then, explicitly use sources across the spectrum and take advantage of looking at how different sources examine the same current event topic.

> **Sources with Limited Bias**
>
> - Scholastic News for elementary school students.
> - Newsela for middle school and high school students.
> - BBC One-Minute World News

4. **Ensuring student understanding.** Model how to determine key ideas and details, identify biases, and prepare for conversation about a source. Support students as they practice these moves independently. The following can help guide this process:
    - Annotate the text with markers for important ideas, questions, or statements that evoke strong emotion.
    - Use a graphic organizer to keep track of key ideas and details.
    - Co-create a list of words that may be indicators of bias.

5. **Preparing for conversation.** Whether taking in a source on the spot or giving ample time to read or view before engaging in conversation, the following can help all students feel comfortable contributing:
    - Develop routine guiding questions that help students get warmed up for the conversation. These may be linked to students' annotations of a source and could include:
        ○ What was the main idea?
        ○ Tell some details that support the main idea.
        ○ What sentence or phrase stood out to you?
        ○ What questions do you have?
    - Ask students to react to what they have read:
        ○ How big of a deal is this issue? Why?
        ○ What personal connections do you have to this issue?
        ○ What biases do you bring to this issue?
        ○ What bias do you note in the source, and how does it impact your thinking about this issue?

> You have to take it from an educational standpoint. When I discussed the election with my students, I asked, "What does voting mean? Why are we voting?" We talked about the candidates and we talked about their policies so we could make informed decisions.
>
> —Marissa Herrera

○ What do you want to know from a person who thinks differently about this issue?

6. **Stay on topic.** Sometimes our conversations can go on a tangent. What constitutes a tangent and when a tangent is a teachable moment is subjective, so decide in the moment whether the conversation needs to be redirected. You can help students (and yourself) stay on topic by:
   - Writing the topic on the whiteboard and reminding students that this is the topic.
   - Including an image that represents the topic.
   - Listing key questions to guide the conversation.
   - Assigning the role of "Topic Manager" to a student.

7. **Know when to keep going.** Sometimes the conversation is so powerful and so important that you need to make the choice to give more time to it. When students are engaged in meaningful conversation that is deepening their understanding of issues, it may be worth sacrificing your lesson plan to keep that going. If students are engaged, go with it and make connections to the ideas raised and skills developed when you return to other lessons.

8. **Know when to wrap up.** When students are getting repetitive or moving into tangents, it may be time to wrap up. Give students a chance to have the last word. Some methods to helps the conversation conclude are:
   - Call on two or three students to summarize what they heard and share their connections or ideas.
   - Ask any students who still want to share to write their ideas down on index cards or white boards. Collect these to review.
   - Find a way to integrate the current event topic and discussion into your curriculum that day or in a future lesson.

   > Let the talkative students know that you value when they give others the floor. They appreciate that you acknowledge they tried hard to give space for their peers to share their opinions.
   >
   > —*Marissa Herrera*

9. **Connect with parents or guardians.** Discussing current events may mean exposing students to viewpoints that differ from what they are learning at home. Stay open about these conversations with students' parents and guardians.
   - Send a letter home at the start of the year letting parents and guardians know that you will be discussing current events. Share some of the framework from this chapter to help them understand the parameters you will set in the classroom.

   > By giving students a small bite [of current events], it encourages them to go out and find more. If I don't include current events in my class on any given day, students complain. Some will seek it out themselves and even post articles on their social media feed. I really like when they start having conversations with their parents about the news. By "Back-to-School Night," I often have parents coming in and talking about the impact.
   >
   > —*Adam Klempa*

- Share some of the ideas and feelings that students write or express verbally and ask parents/guardians about following up.

Considering Different Types of Learners

Though each of the adaptations are likely to benefit all students, the "X" marks indicate adaptations to this strategy that are particularly helpful for English-language learners, Special Education students, and Gifted and Talented students.

_	English-Language Learners			
Provide visuals	Label materials in multiple languages	Translate instructions/ materials to their primary language	Model expectations/ processes	Invite students to write/speak in primary language
X		X	X	X
Special Education Students				
Scaffold instructions/ chunking	Provide positive reinforcement	Schedule breaks	Offer multiple options/formats for student to choose	Minimize distractions
X	X		X	X
Gifted and Talented Students				
Encourage students to focus on learning rather than grades	Celebrate nonacademic successes with students	Provide opportunities for students to take individualized ownership of learning	Challenge students to use more sophisticated vocabulary	Invite students to share how their thinking is extended by hearing new perspectives
		X	X	X

STRATEGY IN ACTION: CURRENT EVENTS AND POETRY

In 2021, my 3rd graders and I watched parts of the US presidential inauguration. My students came from homes that supported this new president as well as homes where their caretakers had voted for another candidate. When introducing the inauguration, I focused on the importance of honoring the leaders of our country and the tradition of this transfer of power. The students all shared an appreciation of the people who came together for the inauguration and for the ceremony itself. We agreed that it was great that so many people were there to share their talents. The students were mesmerized by Amanda Gorman, the country's first Youth Poet Laureate. After watching her speak, we talked about the message she shared and the way that she crafted it with rhyming, rhythm, hand gestures, and her tone of speech. A couple of weeks later, we were talking about poetry, and the students asked to see the video of Amanda Gorman speaking at the inauguration again! I had just wanted to talk about the president and the ceremony, but the students took it to another place. They hadn't seen the inauguration at home, so it was a special time to share it with them, and it led to them not only understanding the traditions of our country, but igniting a passion for poetry!

—*Marissa Herrera*

WHY I LIKE THIS STRATEGY

Sharing *BBC One-Minute World News* with my students takes minimal time and has maximum impact on getting students interested in finding out more about world events. For many students, it's the most consistent exposure that they have to the news, and as they take in this information throughout the year, the number of students who engage in discussion increases exponentially.

—*Adam Klempa*

At 3rd grade, students are still learning how to hold back and how to share. Discussing current events helps them to do this. I get to be a coach for them by removing judgement as we work together to form positive social norms for conversation.

—*Marissa Herrera*

How to Implement the Strategy at Varied Grade Levels

Elementary	Middle	High
*Use sources that are concise and clear. *Rely on videos more than texts, particularly with younger grades. *Encourage students to practice active listening and taking turns in the conversation.	*Differentiate sources to show multiple viewpoints. *Continue to encourage the soft skills of conversation, especially when students do not agree with one another's viewpoints.	*Let students lead the discussion and choose topics of focus that matter to them. *Support students in considering bias of sources and balancing their media intake.

Adaptation for Different Assets and Needs

Time

Limited Time

*If students have more to share, encourage them to write their ideas on a whiteboard or piece of paper and give it to you to review.

*Make time outside of class to continue the conversation. Students might come to sit with you and discuss, or they can make a plan to discuss among themselves during lunch or recess.

Lots of Time

*Create *Go Beyond* options for students who want to learn more. Provide access to sources that represent varied viewpoints. Share images that students can analyze.

*Make it a consistent part of your weekly routine and set aside time that allows students to learn about, be exposed to, analyze, and discuss current events from multiple perspectives.

Cultural Diversity

Limited Diversity

*Have students consider how people with different experiences, values, and needs might see the topics you are discussing.

*Be purposeful about including multiple perspectives in the information that you share.

Lots of Diversity

*Encourage students to share how their experiences and cultures impact their viewpoints and understanding of events.

*Challenge students to consistently see and analyze current events from at least one other perspective presented during class and compare and contrast it with their own viewpoint.

STRATEGY IN ACTION: WHAT'S HAPPENING IN YOUR WORLD

I'd been trying for years to integrate current events into my social studies classrooms. It always seemed a struggle finding something that could fit within the time parameters of my class, but also be impactful enough to have meaning for the students in relation to the curriculum. I tried one year making Fridays *Current Event Day* by having students pull material from the news and presenting in class by giving some level of contextual background and meaningful connection about the event, but it just ended up with students putting something together at the last minute that often lacked the proper context and strained to find connection to the content. It always took more time than I wanted to dedicate and there was little evidence that students were looking at events from a broader perspective.

One year while I was observing a teacher at another school, I noticed he was using the *BBC One-Minute News* in his classroom and it struck me that this could be the right tool. When I asked the teacher about it, he mentioned that he occasionally used it when he noticed there was something in the news that connected to the curriculum; however, I felt this could make a great tool itself. When I returned to my school, I began to integrate it into my class immediately.

I spend one minute on the video and another four minutes answering questions about context and connection, and having students contribute what they know—five minutes each class on some of the most important and pertinent current events. It's always a little slow at the beginning of the year, but over the course of the class, students begin to see the throughlines of news stories as they develop daily; students even start seeking out more information themselves on events that they feel are important. And my favorite benefit aside from the immediate application to the content as it happens in the real world is that students often tell me how they also begin engaging with their parents about not only current events, but how those events relate to the material in the class.

The benefit of the video being from the BBC is that the news has an international focus and doesn't tend to be over-sensationalized like much of American media. It also creates an opportunity for almost every member of my ethnically and culturally diverse class to have a way to relate and contribute.

It's been nine years and I still use this strategy every day in every class. The students love it, and almost all of them say that it's one of their favorite parts of the class.

—Adam Klempa

Sample Materials

Current Events Letter Home

Dear Parent/Guardian,

    I am excited to share with you that our class will be engaging in discussions about current events this year. It is so important for students to develop a strong understanding of what is happening within their local, national, and global community. Having this understanding provides a strong foundation for students' academic work. They can consider how the knowledge and skills they are developing relate to the information they are learning about current events. When you were in school, did you ever ask, "Why do I have to learn this?" Connecting to current events provides strong reasoning for the response to that question!

    The purpose of discussing current events is not about getting the class to align with one way of thinking. Among the many skills that discussing current events supports, respecting multiple perspectives is one of the most important. Please be assured that all points of view are welcome in our classroom. We have set classroom agreements related to respecting others, giving students equitable time to share, and listening with an open mind.

> Below are a few sample topics that we will discuss:
> [TOPIC]

> Below are some sample sources that we will utilize:
> [SOURCES]

If you have any questions or if you have some examples of how this has impacted conversations at home, please reach out to me at [CONTACT INFO].

Best,

[NAME]

Current Events Letter Home
Authors

STRATEGY 20: SUPPORTING STUDENT-LED LEARNING

> Teacher Contributors
> *Revathi Balakrishnan, Elsa England Elementary (TX), 5th grade*
> *Anthony Cianciarulo, Grace A. Dunn Middle School (NJ), 7th–8th grades*

Supporting student-led learning is the process of facilitating students taking ownership of and directing their own learning. Teachers create exposure opportunities to content and skills and then let students explore those ideas on their own while the teacher guides them through the learning and creation of a product that shows mastery; students determine how they will learn and their learning products.

Strategy Implementation

For student-led learning to be successful, it is important to teach students *how* to take ownership of their learning before they take the lead. Then it is important to provide guidance as needed.

Part I: Laying the Foundation

Student-led learning may be new and intimidating to many students. Therefore, take time to lay a strong foundation from the beginning of your school year.

1. **Establish the mindset.** Students may be stuck in a mindset that learning is supposed to be teacher-directed and students are the receptacles of that learning. Therefore, you may need to explicitly and actively work with students to change their mindset to embrace student-led learning. To do this, emphasize:
    - *It's OK to Struggle:* Students need to know it is OK to struggle as they take more ownership of their learning. Let students know that guidance will be given, but not the answers, and they will be supported in attempting to find and uncover answers. Ensure the struggle itself, and everyone struggling together, is celebrated!
    - *Learning Is Not for Grades:* Tell and show students that student-led learning is about the *process* and *taking risks* and *not* about grades.

> **Students May Not Like the Struggle—And That's OK!**
>
> They freakin' hate it and it's OK. They will question you as a teacher as it's your job to give the answer . . . then you try to give every example you have, like when someone picks up the control and plays the game for you. . . . You won't get satisfaction if someone just gives you the answer.
>
> —*Anthony Cianciarulo*

> When you tell students that this is not for a grade, that we're just talking . . . immediately, you can see their shoulders go down and they're relaxed and they're willing to take some risks.
>
> —*Revathi Balakrishnan*

> **Start before Day 1 with Supply Drop Off**
>
> When my 5th-grade students arrive, they are told to find a spot and get their supplies. I watch and tell parents not to help. There are 10 instructions on the board and most students struggle with more than two. The purpose of this exercise is to focus on helping students learn to read the instructions. When students come to me struggling, I ask them, "Is there someone else doing the same things as you that you can ask for help?" Fostering that community while being firm, I am reinforcing that I am not going to help you because everyone needs to learn from mistakes and students can figure it out. If a student finishes, I ask them to help others.
>
> —*Revathi Balakrishnan*

- *Taking Ownership:* It's a process teaching students how to take ownership of student-led learning where you can continually give them success to build on. Start small and get them comfortable with it and then push them more and enable them to thrive and excel with it. Help students move away from *actively not-learning* where they avoid working intentionally, and help students shift toward taking ownership of their learning and celebrate all of the little successes!

2. **Community building.** Student-led learning works when there is collective buy-in from your class, which is directly related to a strong classroom climate and community (see *Strategy 8: Team Building Games* for options). Start community building at the beginning of the year and work to sustain it throughout the year. Once you have done team building games and laid groundwork for a strong community in your classroom, help students work on:
    - *Talking with One Another:* Students need to learn to talk and work with peers from different backgrounds.
    - *Groupings:* Be creative with groupings and empower students to create their own groups while being inclusive of everyone. (See ideas for grouping in *Strategy 17: Peer-to-Peer Relationships and Trust*.)
    - *Modeling:* Student-led learning will come easier to some students than others. Therefore, modeling how to engage in student-led learning makes a big difference in making the process accessible. This modeling can be part of a workshop or separate from it. Different parts of the process you might model include:
        ◦ *Research:* Depending on the age group, content, and comfort level with technology, how you model the research process will differ. Some core elements or research that can be modeled include:

> They can sit by friends, but the only condition in the class is that there can be no kid begging to be part of a team. . . . If someone doesn't have a team, I point it out and all the teams say "come to my team" and then the kid feels wanted. Let students know that "in our class, the expectation is that everyone is included no matter what!"
>
> —*Revathi Balakrishnan*

- Finding and vetting resources
- Annotating and summarizing information from information found
- Interpreting data

- ○ *Comfort with the Freedom of Choice:* For many students, the freedom to choose content, process, or product is scary. Demystify this and practice by modeling small choices you make, talking through how different choices are OK and have value.
- ○ *Questioning/Inquiry:* A key element of student-led learning is students knowing how to engage in inquiry. Model how you create great questions and how those questions lead toward inquiry and investigation of your content.
- ○ *Collaboration and Sharing:* Collaboration and sharing are critical for students to support and push each other with their learning. Show students different ways to collaborate as well as how to share and convey ideas to others; additionally, this is a great place to model how to be great listeners and collaborators when others are sharing their ideas where everyone feels safe and good about the dialogue.

> My job is to make sure your child has enough resources or knows where to go so they are not waiting around for me. . . . it's not going to come easy, but they are going to have to step up and ask the questions they need answered and know where to go to find answers.
>
> —Revathi Balakrishnan

> To teach this, when you read aloud, screw up words on purpose, and talk through how students reacted . . . then go over how they should navigate that in the future. It's about presenting skills and not the content.
>
> —Anthony Cianciarulo

- *Teacher's Role:* Your main job with student-led learning is to maintain the climate and culture of the classroom and provide support and scaffolding for the students throughout the learning process.

3. **Practice resourcefulness and gradual release.** Resourcefulness is essential to student-led learning; help students know how to identify and navigate various resources. This is a process that should employ a gradual release of responsibility, where you provide more support for your students finding the best resources initially and then gradually challenge them to do so without your input and feedback.

4. **Manage classroom routines.** From the outset, help students take ownership of classroom routines including classroom setup and cleanup, transitions, etc. (See

> **Help Students Find Their Best Resources**
>
> Suppose you don't know what to do; what are your resources? They are your friends, books, parents, teacher, internet. What is the hierarchy of that? The teacher should be #4 in the hierarchy of those resources. You are wasting your learning time if you are waiting around for the teacher. Students should see that the teacher is more interested in *them* learning.
>
> —Revathi Balakrishnan

> ### STRATEGY IN ACTION: STUDENT-LED MUSEUM DAY
>
> After a conversation with my students about what history means to them, we decided a museum is the best representation of history for them. So, the plan was to create a museum for our upcoming standards: The cultural contributions of Muslim Society from Muhammad to the Battle to Grenada. Student interest was peaked when they realized they could make projects about math, science, and clothing. These topics are not always covered in detail in my class but were more to their liking than dates and battles.
>
> Initially setting students up with starting research, they went to work with two main goals: (1) Representing the contributions of Muslim Society, and (2) Showing how those contributions are still present in the society the students experience today. Their options for products were quite large from art exhibits to PowerPoints to even podcasts or videos. While most groups made PowerPoints, there was one video and some beautiful posters. A funny aside is one group made a model and were so excited when I told them I would print out their placard on this fancy paper I had. They thought it legitimized their effort to have their words on resume paper. It made them work harder to make sure it was going to look perfect.
>
> Once the projects were done, we had a museum day, and as I would on a field trip, I gave students a guide they had to fill out as they explored the exhibits. Half the class acted as tourists while the other half acted as museum guides, and then they switched. Finally, we had a class discussion on how much we still use items and ideas from that era.
>
> —*Anthony Cianciarulo*

Strategy 2: Establishing Routines and *Strategy 9: Classroom Jobs*). Also, help students communicate their learning with their parents. This helps to reinforce that every element of the students' learning experience and environment is guided by them.

Part II: Implementing Student-Led Learning

Once the groundwork has been laid for student-led learning, it is important to consistently implement it and find ways to adapt how you support students through the process.

1. **Plant seeds and curate materials.** When introducing new materials to students, it is important to provide them with problem posing questions, tidbits of information, or enticing ideas that peak their interest, but don't give them too much! You can curate materials to start their learning journey, but leave the work to the students.
   - *Types of Seeds to Plant:* Provide materials or questions that intrigue and give students enough to latch onto but that can be taken in multiple directions; the journey is about students exploring interests in their own way or collaboratively.
   - *How to Curate Materials:* Create a structure for the work that acts as a road map for students. Provide ending goals (e.g., learning objectives, summative

assessments, etc.) and starting points (e.g., resources that introduce students to and excite them about the topic), but let students figure out their path to those goals. Starting points might include a few examples, links to websites to peak their interest, or a list of curated sites to begin their research. When determining how to curate and scaffold material, consider:
   ○ Making the goal achievable; students need to feel they can reach the goal; otherwise, they are likely not to try.
   ○ How many clues you should give students to reach the end goal on their own.
   ○ Not giving students too much; what you don't give them is more important than what you give them.

2. **Timing and pacing.** Determine how long you have for the unit or project and explicitly communicate it with the students. Let students collaborate in determining the pacing of what they need to do to achieve the goals (e.g., students who created the Museum Day had one week to create exhibits that represented Muslim society and connections to general society today). Students should have a rough pacing and benchmark guide with milestones for them to meet on their way to the end goals; these can be co-created with the students (e.g., students took two days to research their topics and three days to create their museum exhibits). You have the option to use a blended or flipped classroom to meet your timing and pacing needs and let students decide what and how much homework is needed each day.

3. **Consistent implementation.** To maintain student-led learning within your classroom, you need to consistently implement it. Stay active the whole time as a facilitator and mentor, and stay committed to supporting students' independence.
   - *Be Present:* When students are engaged in learning activities, consistently work the room (see *Strategy 12: Working the Room* for ideas) and touch base with each group and student, see where and how they need support, and guide (but don't lead) them.
   - *Support Navigating Roadblocks and Celebrate Small Victories:* When students hit a roadblock; you don't want them to get frustrated and give up. Work on building their capacity to work through those roadblocks so eventually they can do so on their own. When students have success navigating through a roadblock (even a small one), celebrate and reinforce the steps they took! As Anthony Cianciarulo said, "Students are doing it weirdly independently and together with the teacher."
   - *Differentiation and Groupings:* Determine how you want to organize, group, and support your students. Offer a mixture of homogeneous and heterogeneous groupings and provide differentiation to support each of your students. Consider:
     ○ Offering multiple pathways at varying levels of difficulty for students to explore where students can choose to push themselves as much as they think is right. Students want to be challenged and know themselves well, so if multiple options are presented to them, they will likely choose the path that challenges them. Consider opening up to your students about your own vulnerabilities and struggles to create and maintain this open and supportive culture. Then, let students know:

- You will get the support you need.
- In our classroom, we are OK with needing help.
- Things take different amounts of time for everyone, and that's OK!
  - Mix up groups often. Support *each* group while also giving students space to make their own choices and mistakes.
  - Encourage students to get help from others in the room; it shows they are willing to use their resources.
  - Have different levels of goals, so students who finish earlier than others can do a quick assessment with you and then move to the next level of the goals.
  - Have consistent check-ins with groups and individuals throughout the process and at each benchmark where students engage in healthy talk around what they have learned and what they deem the "correct" answers.
- *Working with Disengaged Learners:* Even with the most engaging classroom environment, you may encounter students who choose not to do the work. Find ways to engage them and make learning relevant to their lives.
  - Conference with the student and determine *why* they are not engaging in the work and what can be done to engage them.
  - Provide more individualized attention to the student.
  - Emphasize that they are part of a team with student-led learning. As Anthony Cianciarulo put it, "Students want to be part of something and want structure . . . they don't want to let their team down."

4. **Generate and monitor buy-in.** To maintain student-led learning, you need to monitor buy-in. You can do this by:
   - Looking for that "spark in the eye." Ensure students have and keep their interest in what they are learning.
   - Celebrate what students have achieved throughout the process. Do this verbally and by displaying their work around the classroom.
   - Establish buy-in with *agency* and student *choice*. Allow students to look into things they are most passionate about.
   - Make sure students are *having fun*!

Long-Term Benefits of Student-Led Learning

Because of student-led learning, students are:

- Used to thinking for themselves and coming up with their own ideas that they bring into every part of the lesson, which eliminates the "dead air."
- Able to read, analyze, and contribute on their own and be OK with being "partially right" and working through complicated answers.
- Self-assured with educational tasks: assignments, project, and assessments.

> **STRATEGY IN ACTION: USING CURRENT EVENTS TO SUPPORT STUDENT-LED LEARNING**
>
> I like to use current events in my reading classroom. This past year, one of the articles that I assigned was about Ruth Bader Ginsberg (RBG). We had learned about her in the context of being a pioneer for women. Soon after, she passed away, and I found the opportunity to talk to the students again about her and what a loss it was for women everywhere and how we can carry on her legacy.
>
> I used this opportunity to teach the process of choosing her replacement. Since our Social Studies unit was about the three branches of government, I asked the students to watch whatever news channel they watched to track the progress of the president nominating a judge and the legislature confirming the replacement. After that, the students wanted time in class every morning to talk about the developments in the process the previous day. So, I carved out the time for some robust conversations.
>
> At the end of all of this, I asked the students to talk to their parents about RBG. Many of them told me that they had to educate their parents, and of course, their parents were stunned that their children could talk so much about political processes.
>
> —*Revathi Balakrishnan*

> The beauty of this strategy is that it is as individualized as possible and if you're doing those things and making necessary modifications, then hopefully they should be able to succeed. . . . You just might need to put in more effort as a teacher. It's about the time, effort, and support you provide as a teacher versus the actual difficulty of the project.
>
> —*Anthony Cianciarulo*

Considering Different Types of Learners

Though each of the adaptations are likely to benefit all students, the "X" marks indicate adaptations to this strategy that are particularly helpful for English-language learners, Special Education students, and Gifted and Talented students.

English-Language Learners				
Provide visuals	Label materials in multiple languages	Translate instructions/ materials to their primary language	Model expectations/ processes	Invite students to write/speak in primary language
X	X	X	X	X
Special Education Students				
Scaffold instructions/ chunking	Provide positive reinforcement	Schedule breaks	Offer multiple options/formats for student to choose	Minimize distractions
X	X	X	X	X
Gifted and Talented Students				
Encourage students to focus on learning rather than grades	Celebrate nonacademic successes with students	Provide opportunities for students to take individualized ownership of learning	Challenge students to use more sophisticated vocabulary	Invite students to share how their thinking is extended by hearing new perspectives
X	X	X	X	X

How to Implement the Strategy at Varied Grade Levels

Elementary	*Middle*	*High*
*Limit the number of resources students need to use. *Provide more scaffolding and support for students. *Spend more time on skill building.	*Increase the number of resources students need to use. *Require students to find more of their own resources and choose between which resources they want. *Challenge students to look at things from more than one perspective.	*Put more onus on the students to have them analyze content from new perspectives and in larger contexts. *Let students take the lead from the outset. *Connect learning goals to students' lived experiences and future ambitions.

> ## WHY I LIKE THIS STRATEGY
>
> Students are smart enough to know what they want. This gives them the independence to plan their learning. By giving them the curriculum for each unit, they have a goal they know they must attain. I always tell them at the beginning of the year, when they arrive as new 5th graders, "Now I am looking after you. The goal is that at the end of 5th grade, you should be looking after me." They all laugh, but it happens yearly. Their parents are amazed about how they handle every aspect of the classroom. I know this works because every year, the most often repeated feedback from the students is how much they appreciated the freedom in my class and parents talk about how independent they have become at home.
>
> —*Revathi Balakrishnan*
>
> Humans are most satisfied with themselves when they create. The sense of ownership and pride that comes from being able to claim their hard work culminated into something tangible and shareable creates investment in the skills used to create it. This helps students feel confident and successful using technology, reading, and writing—enjoying the fruits of their labor.
>
> —*Anthony Cianciarulo*

Adaptation for Different Assets and Needs

Size of Class	
Small Class *Limit your interactions with students so you don't disrupt students' flow and progress. *Continuously encourage students to pursue help from their peers before seeking help from you.	**Large Class** *Get something concrete done every day. *Spend less, but targeted time with each student.

Time	
Limited Time *Focus on curating materials and goals that push students based on where they are. *Focus on how to challenge students' ideas and beliefs by focusing on different forms of students' diverse interests and backgrounds.	**Lots of Time** *Work independently with students to set achievable goals and create plans for how to get there (like going from a 2nd-grade reading level to a 5th-grade reading level). *Projects can be catered to each student with individualized rubrics based on each student's goals and needs.

Chapter Five

10 Bonus Strategies

In these final pages, you will find 10 bonus strategies that require small steps for implementation but make a huge impact. Sometimes, teacher candidates and newer teachers benefit from having these teacher moves made explicit. For more seasoned teachers, some of these strategies may seem like teacher moves that are second nature, and if that is the case, hopefully seeing them on this list serves as an affirmation of good practice!

1. **Cabinet of Needs**
   When your students enter the classroom, they enter with different basic needs. Some students are more open about their needs, and others are more reticent to share. Therefore, consider collecting essentials students might need for both personal and academic care and making them available in a cabinet or drawer in your classroom where students can take what they need when they need it. These items might include: bandages, deodorant, snacks, toothbrush and toothpaste, or pencils or markers.

2. **Good Calls Home**
   Teachers often communicate with their students' families when students are struggling or have gotten in trouble. As a result, families come to fear calls home because they assume it is for something bad. To build your students up and celebrate their successes, attempt to make a good call home for each of your students at least once per term. If making that many phone calls is not feasible because of time, inadequate contact information, or other reasons, find another form of communication (e.g., email, text, Class Dojo, etc.) for sending good messages home.

3. **Getting Students' Attention**
   It is important, as a class, to determine signals to get the entire class's attention. This can include signals such as: a call and response, flickering the lights, or claps. Once the class agrees on a signal they like, practice it until you get buy-in from everyone and reinforce it every day. If the chosen signal stops working consistently, come up with a new signal with the class to keep it relevant and meaningful.

4. **Class Playlist**
   Music can help transform your classroom environment, provide renewed energy, necessary calming, or act as a signal for transitions. At the start of the year, survey your students to learn their favorite songs and then compile a class playlist (with *radio* versions of the songs) that you play in your classroom. When students hear their favorite song, it will excite them and make them feel seen and honored within your classroom. Ask for students to share new favorite songs periodically throughout the year.

5. **Student of the Week**
   Every student deserves to be celebrated! Select a different student every week to honor. Set aside time for them to share artifacts from their life, choose an activity they love to do with the class, and be praised by the class for accomplishments (academic and nonacademic). Consider having them fill out a survey that's read to the class about their likes and having the class make a book for them (each student fills out a page) with compliments about the Student of the Week. This helps create a culture of fun, love, and appreciation.

6. **Public Boosts**
   As you learn more about your students and keep up with their activities and accomplishments inside and outside the classroom, give each student a public boost by letting the rest of the class know the great things that students are doing. Some students might be shy and not love the attention; therefore, give them a heads up that you want to give them a public boost and ask for their consent to do so. Try to equitably highlight every student over the course of the year.

7. **Student Quote Wall of Fame**
   Create a student quote Wall of Fame on a bulletin board. At the beginning of the year, let students know to pay attention to amazing things their peers say, and then come up with a system for students to identify and post their favorite student quotes on the Wall of Fame. Consider having a short ceremony for each new quote added where the student who said the quote says it out loud to the class, the student who nominated or posted the quote explains why they love it, and the rest of the class can give a positive affirmation of the student's choosing.

8. **Students Become Teachers**
   To truly make your classroom climate student-centered, create space and opportunities for students to become teachers, for you and their peers. Students can teach the class about something they are an expert in (e.g., culture, passions, knowledge, or skills) or you can design activities related to your curriculum where students learn a concept or skill and teach their peers.

9. **Prepping to Talk about the Day Outside of School**
   Classroom climate is enhanced and reinforced when students share with their families what they are doing in your class. Young students in particular might need support in how best to talk about their day. Work with students during your conclusion activity to have students summarize their main takeaways from lesson(s), elements they loved and why they loved them, and questions they still have. Then, have your students practice explaining this to the class as a rehearsal for sharing at home.

10. **Greetings and Goodbyes**
    Together with your students, develop a class greeting and a class goodbye. These might be phrases that you say, a clever handshake, or even a song that students sing to start and end the day together. These greetings and goodbyes personalize the shared class experience and provide emotional cues that it is time to come together as a class or transition into what's next.

Conclusion

This book was developed as a resource that would be useful for *all* teachers in *all* settings. Hopefully the details in the step-by-step description of the strategies help you to make your classroom community a positive, safe, vulnerable, and brave space.

NOW WHAT?

Remember to take a culturally responsive/sustaining approach to using these strategies. To do this, ask yourself:

- What do I know about my students?
- How can I adapt these strategies to best fit my students' learning needs?

Further, be sure to integrate these strategies with clear intention and explicit explanation of *why* you are doing what you are doing. Sharing the *why* will help students get on board with you and, more importantly, help them think critically about the type of *classroom climate* they want to build together. After trying a new strategy, take time to reflect. Consider:

- What worked well?
- Why did these elements succeed?
- What changes might I make?
- How could I adapt the strategy to better fit my needs or my students' needs?

Most strategies will need to be adapted in some way to fit your classroom. Hopefully the adaptations listed in each strategy are helpful in guiding your thinking. You might consider applying an adaptation from one chapter to a strategy in another chapter. If you are struggling with how to change a strategy, reach out to a colleague, ask your students, or connect with fellow educators at:

Website: https://buildyourteachingtoolbox.com/
Twitter: @BuildTeachTool
Instagram: @buildteachingtoolbox
Facebook: Build Your Teaching Toolbox

AND THEN?

Practice! Practice! Practice! How do you get better at anything? You practice! Practice new strategies until you feel confident using them in your classroom. Practice adapting strategies. Practice reaching out to colleagues for support, advice, or to be cheered on for your efforts.

Perhaps you are reading this book and thinking, "Hey! I've got some great strategies that can be adapted for varied classroom settings! How do I get my ideas in a book?" Glad you asked! Please, join the toolbox sharing community at:

Website: https://buildyourteachingtoolbox.com/
Email: buildyourteachingtoolbox@gmail.com
Twitter: @BuildTeachTool
Instagram: @buildteachingtoolbox
Facebook: Build Your Teaching Toolbox

Remember, this is the second book in the five-book *Building Your Teaching Toolbox* series! Check out *Adaptable Teaching: 30 Practical Strategies for All School Contexts*, and be on the lookout for our upcoming books, each of which will focus on a deep dive into a different key area of teaching (i.e., planning, instruction, and professional development).

All books in this series will include step-by-step instructions for implementing and applying strategies, narratives of the Strategy in Action, teacher explanations of why they like each strategy, examples of how to modify the strategy based on related assets and needs, and modifications based on grade level (i.e., elementary, middle, high) and different populations of students (i.e., Special Education, English-language learners, and Gifted and Talented).

In addition to creating a book that could be a strong resource for teachers in varied settings and at different points in their career, this book was written with the hope that it would draw you in as readers and help you feel like a part of a larger community of educators who are eager to share and grow together. Please keep the community growing by providing feedback and new ideas at the email address, website, or social media platforms for the *Building Your Teaching Toolbox* community. Thank you for joining the toolbox community!

References

ASCD. (2019, March 16). Students have to Maslow before they can Bloom. *Twitter*. https://twitter.com/ascd/status/1106937108940406789?lang=en

Bear, G. G. (2015). Preventive and classroom-based strategies. In E. T. Emmer & E. J. Sabornie (Eds.), *Handbook of classroom management* (2nd ed., pp. 15–39). Routledge.

Bloom, B. S. (1956). *Taxonomy of educational objectives, handbook I: The cognitive domain*. David McKay Co. Inc.

Boykin, A. W., & Noguera, P. (2011). *Creating the opportunity to learn: Moving from research to practice to close the achievement gap*. Association for Supervision and Curriculum Development.

Cartledge, G., Lo, Y., Vincent, C. G., & Robinson-Ervin, P. (2015). Culturally responsive classroom management. In E. T. Emmer & E. J. Sabornie (Eds.), *Handbook of classroom management* (2nd ed., pp. 411–30). Routledge.

Costal, A., & Kalick, B. (2008). *16 Habits of Mind*. ASCD.

Darling Hammond, L. (2015). Want to close the achievement gap? Close the teaching gap. *American Educator, 38*(4), 14–18.

Davis, J. R. (2017). *Classroom management in teacher education programs*. Palgrave Macmillan.

Davis, J. R. & Connolly, M. (2022). *Adaptable teaching: 30 practical strategies for all school contexts*. Rowman & Littlefield.

Dennison, P. E., & Dennison, G. E. (1994). *Brain gym: Simple activities for whole brain learning*. Edu Kinesthetics.

Duncan-Andrade, J. (2011). *Growing roses in concrete*. TEDxGoldenGateED, September 28, 2011. https://www.youtube.com/watch?v=2CwS60ykM8s

Elias, M. J., Zins, J. E., Weissberg, R. P., et al. (1997). *Promoting social and emotional learning: Guidelines for educators*. ASCD. https://earlylearningfocus.org/wp-content/uploads/2019/12/promoting-social-and-emotional-learning-1.pdf

Gay, G. (2010). *Culturally responsive teaching: theory, research, and practice* (2nd ed.). Teachers College Press.

Ginott, H. (1972). *Between teacher and child*. Macmillan.

Gutiérrez, K. D., & Rogoff, B. (2003). Cultural ways of learning: Individual traits or repertoires of practice. *Educational Researcher 32*(5), 19–25. doi:10.3102/0013189x032005019

Gutstein, E., Lipman, P., Hernández, P., & de los Reyes, R. (1997). Culturally relevant mathematics teaching in a Mexican American context. *Journal for Research in Mathematics Education, 28*, 709–37. doi:10.2307/749639

Ladson-Billings, G. (1995). Towards a culturally relevant theory of pedagogy. *American Educational Research Journal, 32*, 465–91.

Lasic, T. (n.d.). Maslow before bloom. *Human Edublogs.* https://human.edublogs.org/2009/08/11/maslow-before-bloom/

Maslow, A. H. (1943). A theory of human motivation. *Psychological Review 4*(50), 370–96.

McLaughlin, J. H., & Bryan, L. A. (2003). Learning from rural Mexican schools about commitment and work. *Theory into Practice, 42*(4), 289–95.

Miller, J. (n.d.). Gotta "Maslow" before you "bloom". *The Educator's Room.* https://theeducatorsroom.com/gotta-maslow-bloom-2/

Paris, D., & Alim, H. S. (eds.). (2017). *Culturally sustaining pedagogies: Teaching and learning for justice in a changing world.* New York: Teachers College Press.

Rist, R. C. (1972). Planned incapacitation: A case study of how not to teach black teachers to teach. *Journal of Higher Education, 43*, 620–35. doi:10.2307/1980839

Silverman, K. *Big talk.* https://www.makebigtalk.com/

Villegas, A. M., & Lucas, T. (2002). *Educating culturally responsive teachers.* Albany: State University of New York Press.

Weiner, L. (2003). Why is classroom management so vexing to urban teachers? *Theory into Practice, 42*, 305–12. doi:.1353/tip.2003.0052

Weiner, L. (2006). Challenging deficit thinking. *Educational Leadership, 64*(1), 42–45.

Weinstein, C. S., Tomlinson-Clarke, S., & Curran, M. (2004). Toward a conception of culturally responsive classroom management. *Journal of Teacher Education, 55*(1), 25–38. doi:10.1177/0022487103259812

Index

academic diversity, 89
Adaptable Teaching (Davis & Connolly), 9, 158
adaptations. *See* different assets and needs in classrooms; elementary school adaptations; English-Language Learners adaptations; gifted and talented student adaptations; high school adaptations; middle school adaptations; special education adaptations; time adaptations
affirmations, 14, 99, 154
    See also Spotlighting Students strategy
Alim, H. S., 4
animal association game, 42
apps, 97
assessment assistant, 63
asset-focused discussions, 47
attendance monitors, 61
attention-getting signals, 153

Balakrishnan, Revathi, 143–51
BBC One-Minute News, 136, 139, 141
behavior charts, 10
Belasco, Thomas (TJ), 97–103
Between Teacher and Child (Ginott), 2
Big Talk (Silverman), 119
BINGO, 45–46, 61
Bloom's Taxonomy, 3
body activities. *See* Brain and Body Breaks strategy
Bokenyi, Brenda, 31–41
"Book Nook," 29, 30
books, 97

Brain and Body Breaks strategy
    adaptations, 93–95
    benefits, 58, 92, 95
    implementing, 90–93, 96
breathing and mindfulness, 98
Bruin babysitters, 61
buy-in of students, 12, 74, 85, 92, 103

cabinet of needs, 153
calisthenics, 91
calming visuals activity, 90
card table topper activity, 119–20, 121
Check-Ins strategy
    adaptations, 69–71
    benefits, 57, 67, 70
    implementing, 35, 67–68, 69, 71
    sample materials, 72
    transitions and, 81
checklists, 35
Cianciarulo, Anthony, 143–51
class photographers, 61
class presidents, 63
classroom culture, 12
classroom design. *See* Room Setup strategy
classroom family, 50
classroom handbook, 33
classroom hosts, 66
classroom houses, 48–51
Classroom Jobs strategy
    adaptations, 64–65
    benefits, 57, 64
    implementing, 60–63, 100
    Job Wheels, 66

classroom library, 24
class size adaptations
    Brain and Body Breaks, 95
    Classroom Jobs, 65
    Peer-to-Peer Relationships and Trust, 127
    Room Setup, 82
    Spotlighting Students, 108
    Student-Led Learning, 151
    Team-Building Games, 53
    Working the Room, 89
Cline, Jennifer Podolak, 81–89
clubs, 103
coaches, 97
collaboration
    for breaks, 92
    community building and, 145
    importance of, 130
    room setup and, 82–83
    for routines, 13
    for written agreements, 10
    See also sharing of information; Working the Room strategy
come back to calm activity, 98–99
comfort zones, 119
community, classroom as, 10, 144–45, 158
    See also classroom houses; introductory slides/posters; Peer-to-Peer Relationships and Trust strategy
Connecting through Current Events strategy
    adaptations, 138, 140
    benefits, 111–12, 139
    implementing, 134–38, 139, 141–42
    See also connection building
connection building, 35, 36–37, 84, 87
    See also Connecting through Current Events strategy; Team-Building Games strategy; Working the Room strategy
critical conversations, 36
Critical Feedback Survey strategy, 18–20
CRP (culturally relevant pedagogy), 4
CRT (culturally responsive/sustaining teaching), 4
cultural diversity, adaptions for, 80, 127, 140
culturally relevant pedagogy (CRP), 4
culturally responsive/sustaining teaching (CRT), 4
current events. See Connecting through Current Events strategy

curriculum and connection, 36–37, 119
Curtin, Andrew, 67–71

debriefing strategies
    for feedback, 19–20
    for introductory slides/posters, 36
    for minutes or minutes gift, 77
    for role plays, 123
    for team-building games, 44, 46
desk configuration, 23, 82
different assets and needs in classrooms
    cultural diversity adaptions, 80, 127, 140
    funding adaptations, 28
    school context, 6
    student personality adaptations, 40, 71, 117
    teacher personality adaptations, 53
    See also class size adaptations; elementary school adaptations; English-Language Learners adaptations; gifted and talented student adaptations; high school adaptations; middle school adaptations; special education adaptations; time adaptations
direct messaging, 85
display space, 23, 24, 25
distractions for reducing stress, 90
diversity of student backgrounds, 80, 127, 140
drumming activity, 90
Duncan-Andrade, Jeff, 3
Dynamic Classroom Management Approach (DCMA), 3–4

Eldredge-Sandbo, Mary, 81–89
electronic device chats, 85
elementary school adaptations
    Brain and Body Breaks, 94
    Check-Ins, 70
    Classroom Jobs, 65
    Connecting through Current Events, 140
    Getting to Know Students, 39
    Mindfulness, 101
    Peer-to-Peer Relationships and Trust, 125
    Room Setup, 27
    Spotlighting Students, 106
    Student-Led Learning, 150
    Students Sharing Thinking and Feelings, 131

Student Voice to Start Class, 79
Teacher-Student Relationships and Trust, 116
Team-Building Games, 52
empathy, 46–48
Empty Pot activity, 128
energizing activities, 90–92
English-Language Learners adaptations
    Brain and Body Breaks, 94
    Check-Ins, 69
    Classroom Jobs, 64
    Connecting through Current Events, 138
    families of, 32
    Getting to Know Students, 38
    Mindfulness, 100
    Peer-to-Peer Relationships and Trust strategy, 126
    Room Setup, 26
    Spotlighting Students, 106
    Student-Led Learning strategy, 150
    Students Sharing Thinking and Feelings strategy, 131
    Student Voice to Start Class, 79
    Teacher-Student Relationships and Trust strategy, 115
    Team-Building Games, 51
    Working the Room, 88
Establishing Routines strategy. *See* routines
extracurriculars, 31, 34, 114

Failing Forward strategy, 16–17, 119
fall break madness/sadness game, 46–48
families of students. *See* home-school communications and connections; home visits
feedback, 62, 105
feelings check-in, 68
    See also Students Sharing Thinking and Feelings strategy
Feurer, Bob, 113–17
fidgets, 91
First, Emma, 128–33
first days of school
    getting to know students, 34–36
    integrating knowledge of students, 36–37
    pre-class surveys/prep, 34
    routines, 12–13
    setting the tone, 118–19
five things activity, 98

food in classrooms, 113
four corners activity, 90–91
Frade, Kristen, 118–27
fresh starts, 114–15, 117
funding, adaptations for, 28
furniture configuration, 23, 82

Gay, Geneva, 4
Getting to Know Students strategy
    adaptations, 37–39, 40
    benefits, 21, 38
    extracurriculars, 31, 34
    first day strategies, 34–36
    integrating knowledge into classroom, 36–37
    sample materials, 41
    See also home visits; Team-Building Games strategy
gifted and talented student adaptations
    Brain and Body Breaks, 94
    Check-Ins, 69
    Classroom Jobs, 64
    Connecting through Current Events, 138
    Getting to Know Students, 38
    Mindfulness, 100
    Peer-to-Peer Relationships and Trust, 126
    Room Setup, 26
    Spotlighting Students, 106
    Student-Led Learning, 150
    Students Sharing Thinking and Feelings, 131
    Student Voice to Start Class, 79
    Teacher-Student Relationships and Trust, 115
    Team-Building Games, 51
    Working the Room, 88
Ginott, Haim, 2
Ginsberg (Ruth Bader) lesson, 149
Goff, Pamela, 90–96
goodbyes, 155
greetings, 14, 81, 155
Griffiths, Jordan, 67–71
grounding activities, 90, 91
Group Agreements strategy, 10–11, 44, 134
groups
    community building and, 144–45
    individual *versus* collaborative breaks, 92
    peer-to-peer trust and, 119–21
    small groups, 93, 129

student-led learning and, 147–48
    work in, 83, 86
growth mindset, 16

hand partner game, 91
Herrera, Marissa, 134–42
heterogeneous groups, 48
high school adaptations
    Brain and Body Breaks, 94
    Check-Ins, 70
    Classroom Jobs, 65
    Connecting through Current Events, 140
    Getting to Know Students, 39
    Mindfulness, 101
    Peer-to-Peer Relationships and Trust, 125
    Room Setups, 27
    Spotlighting Students, 106
    Student-Led Learning, 150
    Students Sharing Thinking and Feelings, 131
    Student Voice to Start Class, 79
    Teacher-Student Relationships and Trust, 116
    Team-Building Games, 52
home-school communications and connections, 37, 137–38, 142, 153, 155
home visits
    adaptations, 37–39, 40
    benefits of, 38, 39
    implementing, 31–34
    using notes from, 37
homework monitors, 61
homogeneous groups, 48
hopscotch, 91
humor, 113–14, 116

independent work, 15
index cards, 85
individual breaks, 93
interviewing peers game, 42–43
introductory slides/posters, 35, 37, 40–41

Klempa, Adam, 134–42

Ladson-Billings, G., 4
Landy, Alyssa, 90–96
Lasic, Tomaz, 3
learning dialogue, 37

Leija, Daniel, 128–33
listening skills, 135, 136
Loving Kindness Practice, 102
Lucas, T., 4

Maslow, A. H., 3
McElrath, Larissa, 23–30
middle school adaptations
    Brain and Body Breaks, 94
    Check-Ins, 70
    Classroom Jobs, 65
    Connecting through Current Events, 140
    Getting to Know Students, 39
    Mindfulness, 101
    Peer-to-Peer Relationships and Trust, 125
    Room Setup, 27
    Spotlighting Students, 106
    Student-Led Learning, 150
    Students Sharing Thinking and Feelings, 131
    Student Voice to Start Class, 79
    Teacher-Student Relationships and Trust, 116
    Team-Building Games, 52
Miller, Jake, 3
mindfulness-based breathing activity, 90
Mindfulness strategy
    adaptations, 100–101, 103
    benefits, 58, 101, 103
    implementing, 97–100, 102, 103
modeling strategies, 46, 67, 74, 114, 128–29, 144–45
movement in the classroom, 83–84
"mug shot" corkboard, 29
museum day, 146
music, 35, 82, 154

name games, 42–43
Neary, Ann, 31–41
note-taking, 33, 83

organizational routines, 12

pair work, 15
Paris, D., 4
pedagogical routines, 13
Peer-to-Peer Relationships and Trust strategy
    adaptations, 125–27

benefits, 111, 122, 127
    groupings, 119–21
    role playing, 121–25, 127
    setting the tone, 118–19
poker chip races, 43–45, 54–55
Positive Affirmations strategy, 14–15, 75, 77
positive climate in classrooms
    benefits, 111–12
    guiding questions, 112
    highlights, 112
    strategies for, 111–12
positivity, 35
posters, 129
practice, 13, 158
procedural routines, 12
profile pages, 107
prompts, 74, 83
puppets, 133

quality control, 62

Raser, Jennifer, 113–17
RBG (Ruth Bader Ginsberg) lesson, 149
readiness check-ins, 68
reading activity, 90
"Reading Graffiti" bulletin board, 29, 30
redos, 123–25
Reed, Dwayne, 3
reflection
    encouraging, 16–17
    on feedback, 20
    on home visits, 33–34
    on poker chip races, 44
    on strategies, 157–58
resourcefulness, 145
Room Setup strategy
    adaptations, 26–28
    benefits of, 21, 26
    implementing, 23–25, 27, 29–30
routines
    assessing and adapting, 13
    for beginning of class, 82
    benefits, 57–58, 73–74
    breaks integrated into, 92
    guiding questions, 59
    highlights, 58
    list of, 57–58
    organizational, 12

    pedagogical, 13
    procedural, 12
    student ownership of, 145–46
    See also Classroom Jobs strategy

safe spaces, 134–35
safety monitors, 61
seating options, 24–25, 26
SEL (social emotional learning), 3, 97, 125
    See also Mindfulness strategy
self-assessments, 16
sharing of information, 7, 74–75, 93, 104–5, 109
    See also collaboration; Students Sharing Thinking and Feelings strategy
show and tell activity, 37
Silverman, Kalina, 119
Simon says activity, 90
size of classes. *See* class size adaptations
skip counting game, 96
small groups, 93, 129
social emotional learning (SEL), 3, 97, 125
    See also Mindfulness strategy
special education adaptations
    Brain and Body Breaks, 94
    Check-Ins, 69
    Classroom Jobs, 64
    Connecting through Current Events, 138
    Getting to Know Students, 38
    Mindfulness, 100
    Peer-to-Peer Relationships and Trust, 126
    Room Setup, 26
    Spotlighting Students, 106
    Student-Led Learning, 150
    Students Sharing Thinking and Feelings, 131
    Student Voice to Start Class, 79
    Teacher-Student Relationships and Trust, 115
    Team-Building Games, 51
    Working the Room, 88
Spotlighting Students strategy
    adaptations, 105–6, 108
    benefits, 58, 107, 109
    implementing, 104–5, 107, 109
stages in the classroom, 27
stress relievers. *See* Brain and Body Breaks strategy

stretching activities, 91
Student-Led Learning strategy
    adaptations, 149–51
    benefits, 112, 148, 149, 151
    implementing, 146–49
    laying the foundation, 143–46
student of the week, 61, 154
students
    adaptations for different personalities, 40, 71, 117
    affirmations for, 15
    feedback from, 19–20
    getting attention of teachers, 85
    greeting, 14, 81, 155
    profile pages for, 107
    quotations from, 154
students become teachers activity, 154
Students Sharing Thinking and Feelings strategy
    adaptations, 130–32
    benefits, 111, 132
    implementing, 128–30, 133
Student Voice to Start Class strategy
    adaptations, 78–80
    author's chair, 73, 74–75
    benefits, 57, 73–74, 78
    connecting with content/theme, 78
    minutes and minute gifts, 76–77
    quick writes, 73–74, 75
Sullivan, Kate, 104–9
supplies/materials, 23
Supply Drop Off activity, 144
supreme court in classrooms, 63
surveys, 18–20, 38, 40
Synder, Allison, 23–29

Take What You Need drawers, 23, 153
teachers
    adaptations for different personalities of, 53
    introductory slides/poster, 35
    moving in the class, 83–84
    sharing interests, 113
    students as, 154
    traveling from room to room, 88
Teacher-Student Relationships and Trust strategy
    adaptations, 115–17
    benefits, 111, 116
    implementing, 113–15
teacher-to-student affirmations, 14
Team-Building Games strategy
    adaptations, 51–53
    beginning-of-year games, 42–46
    benefits of, 21, 45, 47, 52
    check-in games, 46–48
    classroom houses, 48–51
    sample materials, 54–55
technology, 84–85, 104, 129, 132
Ted Talks, 128
temp jobs, 63
themes, 74
think-pair-share activities, 44
time adaptations
    Brain and Body Breaks, 95
    Check-Ins, 71
    Classroom Jobs, 65
    Connecting through Current Events, 140
    Getting to Know Students, 40
    Mindfulness, 103
    Room Setup, 28
    Spotlighting Students, 108
    Student-Led Learning, 151
    Students Sharing Thinking and Feelings, 132
    Student Voice to Start Class, 80
    Teacher-Student Relationships and Trust, 117
time allocations, 19, 147
toolbox sharing, 158
trace hand activity, 91
transitions, 75, 77, 92
traveling teachers, 88
trust, 99
    See also Peer-to-Peer Relationships and Trust strategy; Teacher-Student Relationships and Trust strategy
Tumolo, Anthony, 97–103

videos, 97
Villegas, A. M., 4
visual learning, 84–85
    See also Students Sharing Thinking and Feelings strategy

walking activities, 91, 98

Wall of Fame, 154
Weinstein, C. S., 4
"What happens if...?" considerations, 11
whole-class affirmations, 15
whole-class breaks, 93
whole-class sharing, 129
Wilke, Janice, 104–9
Wilson, Lorin, 118–27

Working the Room strategy
    adaptations, 87–89
    benefits, 58, 89
    implementing, 81–87
Would you rather? activity, 91

yoga activities, 91

www.ingramcontent.com/pod-product-compliance
Lightning Source LLC
Chambersburg PA
CBHW080323020526
44117CB00035B/2636